LIVING LITURGY

By the same author:
  Liturgy and Liberty
  And For Your Children
  Hymns and Spiritual Songs
  Responding to Preaching

Living Liturgy

John Leach

KINGSWAY PUBLICATIONS
EASTBOURNE

ISBN 0 85476 750 9

Co-published in South Africa with
SCB Publishers
Cornelis Struik House, 80 McKenzie Street
Cape Town 8001, South Africa.
Reg no 04/02203/06

Designed and produced by Bookprint Creative Services
P.O. Box 827, BN21 3YJ, England, for
KINGSWAY PUBLICATIONS LTD
Lottbridge Drove, Eastbourne, East Sussex BN23 6NT.
Printed in Great Britain.

Contents

Introduction

My previous book, *Liturgy and Liberty*, on which I began work in 1986, seemed to be fairly well received by those who bought a copy, and some have even been kind enough to say that it really was of practical help in the worship of their own churches. By a strange coincidence it went out of print over the very weekend of the major Worship Together conference in Eastbourne in January 1997, at which nearly 3,000 delegates gathered to seek again God's heart for worship. The whole weekend was a tremendous spiritual experience for me personally, and really did establish firmly some new directions in the worship of charismatic renewal.

But the thing which really struck me was the tremendous interest in the subject of liturgy. I had tried to contribute something, through the writing of *Liturgy and Liberty*, to the debate between those who regarded liturgy as the only way to worship and those who saw it as a tool of the devil to keep us from worship. I also attempted to pass on some of the lessons I had learned as a leader of charismatic worship in an Anglican setting. Suddenly, it seemed, people wanted to hear what it was I had to say. Some negotiation followed a chance encounter at Eastbourne with Chris Jackson, a member of the Kingsway editorial team, and before long we had decided to risk a rewrite.

As I read through *Liturgy and Liberty* again to see what might be salvaged, I was struck by how incredibly out of date it was after only eight years in print. Liturgically the ASB was well established but still had a slightly new and radical feel about it: now it is almost past it, and liturgists are working hard on its replacement for the year 2000. And of course many of the songs I quoted were long dead and forgotten, at least in the circles in which I move. New elements in charismatic spirituality have come powerfully onto the scene: the advent of the 'Toronto blessing' and the urgent hope for and expectation of nationwide revival have radically affected the flavour of our public worship. And my membership of a couple of creative liturgical groups has taught me a tremendous amount more about the official Anglican scene. There is so much more to say than there was in 1989, and a pretty different world into which to say it.

And yet not everything had changed. I was still seeking to work out the vision for worship which I had first articulated while on the staff of St Thomas' Crookes in Sheffield, but now it was as vicar of my own parish in Coventry with a completely new set of musicians and an entirely different liturgical feel to the church. Many of the principles and practices forged in the former rather high-powered setting had transferred successfully to an 'ordinary' parish, and apart from the fact that I had begun to question the theology of worship which *Liturgy and Liberty* expounded, much remained the same and was still, I felt, worth saying again.

Another major weakness of *Liturgy and Liberty* was the fact that nowhere did it actually explain what liturgy is. So that needed to be done, and it needed backing up with some material which explained the value of liturgy to renewed worship – material which first took shape as a keynote address at the GROW Conference 'Evangelicals and Worship Beyond 2000' at Swanwick in January 1997 (what a busy month that was!).

Other material has been superseded, not because it is out of date but because it has been written up more fully elsewhere. The original chapter on 'Children and Worship' became a whole book,[1] and some of the material on change was incorporated into the CPAS pack entitled *At Your Service*.[2] But much has been retained, in an updated form.

Alarmed at how quickly and thoroughly the previous book had dated, I took a policy decision in writing this one that I would avoid wherever possible mentioning specific worship songs. This ought to give it a longer shelf life, but has the down side that it is less specific in describing actual worship moods or progressions. I hope that won't matter too much, and that you'll be able to see what I mean. I am aware also that in some ways this is a really bad time to be writing about liturgy: while I have had some sneak previews of what the Church of England is likely to be using in its worship in the next millennium, very little is fixed at this stage. I could be a lot less vague if I waited three years before writing this, but I feel that there is both an urgent need and a moment of opportunity to be writing now. So I'll hope for the best that the *Gloria in excelsis*, for example, will survive to its 1,650th birthday and still be with us after AD 2000.

For whom is this book intended? For anyone, really, who is involved in the conduct of worship of whatever style. Clergy and ministers, lay people involved in leading worship (such as Anglican Readers), musicians and singers, those involved in planning worship: all may find material here which is relevant to their role. It is still a fact that in the years since the publication of *Liturgy and Liberty* there has been virtually nothing written which helps charismatic Anglicans to lead worship. Everything there is (and precious little at that) comes from a New Church background, and while there is much material which is significantly helpful, there is little or nothing on the subject of liturgy, other than an occasional description of it as 'dead', 'formal', 'empty' and so on (which, of course, it often can be).

It is so sad that most of the history of the church has consisted of throwing babies out with the bathwater, and yet I sense that we are entering a time when there is an increasing desire among charismatics to rescue the liturgical infant just before it swirls entirely down the plughole and out of their sight. It is my conviction more than ever that God is wanting to work because of tradition rather than in spite of it. He will work in spite of it if he needs to, but I believe that would be second best.

So I hope this will be a new book, even though it had its birth eleven years ago and still contains some of the former material. Times have changed, but the debate goes on: what exactly is the best way to worship God? I hope that at the very least I can point in the right direction.

Notes

1 John and Chris Leach, *And for Your Children* (Crowborough: Monarch, 1994).
2 John Leach and Mark Earey, *At Your Service* (Warwick: CPAS, 1997).

1

What Is Worship?

It has been very popular in some circles over the last few years to speak in terms of God 'coming' or 'turning up' as we worship. 'How did it go?' asks my wife as I return home after the evening service. 'Great,' I reply. 'God really showed up!', by which I mean that when I left at 11.30 pm the sanctuary carpet was still littered with bodies, like the aftermath of some major disaster. The motto of the influential Vineyard movement, 'Come, Holy Spirit', and the many songs of invitation to him have reinforced in us an expectation that as we worship, God gets involved by coming to do what he does among us.

I don't really have a problem with this understanding, and in *Liturgy and Liberty* I spent a lot of time building a whole theology of worship around it.[1] I argued there (and I still believe) that there is excellent biblical and liturgical evidence to suggest that 'Come, Holy Spirit' is a perfectly good prayer to pray. Many times in the Old Testament individuals or groups of people experienced the coming upon them of the 'Spirit of the Lord', with all sorts of interesting results. Commonly they began to prophesy, like the elders in Numbers 11:25, Balaam in Numbers 24:2, and several others. Slightly more unlikely people to be affected in this way were Saul in 1 Samuel 10:10, and three companies of his soldiers in 1 Samuel 19:20–21. Sometimes people were anointed for leadership by the Spirit. This happened to several of the Judges, for example Gideon in Judges 6:34, and Kings Saul and David in 1 Samuel 11:6 and 16:13. This continued into the ministry of the prophets later on, notably Ezekiel. Clearly, here was one sense in which God was able to 'come' upon or among people. Perhaps this was a forerunner of what we should expect in worship today, even if the occasional cutting up of oxen or dismembering of young lions which resulted doesn't play a major part in modern-day Anglican liturgy.

It is possible to argue, of course, that all that was in the Old Testament, but we now live in the era of the New. No longer does the Spirit need to 'come upon' us, because through the ministry of Jesus he is now given to live within us. What was for Balaam and his pals a temporary anointing should be for us a constant reality. Dangerous though this would be for oxen and lions, there is truth in it, although my own experience tells me that I'm never too full of the Spirit to need a fresh anointing.

There is, though, in the Old Testament, another type of 'coming' by God among his people, one which is far more closely linked with worship. This is the appearance of the 'glory' (later called the *shekinah*) of God, first on Mount Sinai, then in the desert at the Mosaic tabernacle, and later in Solomon's Temple. This is a difficult concept for us to get hold of, but apparently the people would have been able to see when God was around because of what was described as a cloud, smoke or fire filling the sanctuary. It wasn't so much that God was somehow hidden in the smoke, but rather more that the smoke, like the flag flying on top of Buckingham Palace, was a sign that the King was in residence. When God came and sat enthroned between the golden cherubim on the lid of the ark of the covenant, the cloud of his glory would be clearly visible to the worshippers. This 'glory' is seen in Exodus 16:10 for the first time, and manifests itself often, notably in Exodus 19:18, 40:34 and 1 Kings 8:10.

It is significant that Ezekiel, prophesying about the destruction of Jerusalem, sees in a vision the glory of the Lord leaving the Temple. It becomes the prayer of the despairing psalmist, notably in Psalm 80, that God will once more shine forth from between the cherubim and come to save and restore his people. While there was in later Old Testament spirituality the clear belief that God was omnipresent, there were certainly times when it didn't feel as if he were there, and needed to be urged to 'return' (Ps 80:14), to 'come down' (Is 64:1), or even to 'remember' his people (Ps 74:2). Right at the end of the Old Testament period are some prophecies which anticipate the answer to these prayers, when Zechariah looks forward to the presence of the glory of the Lord in the new Jerusalem (Zech 2:5) and his contemporary, Haggai, speaks of a fresh coming of the Lord to his Temple, filling it with an unprecedented display of his glory, and with peace for the longing worshippers (Hag 2:6–9). In the Old Testament at least, it seemed to be the case that God could and did come among his people.

But what of the New Testament? Surely Jesus was the person in whom God came once and for all? Surely the gift of the Holy Spirit means that there need be no further divine comings and goings? In theory one would perhaps expect this to be true, but a closer look at the Gospels and Acts reveals the same sort of evidence as that which we have found already in the Old Testament. Individuals such as Jesus at his baptism and Stephen at his death were specially anointed by the Spirit (Lk 3:22; Acts 7:55); he came upon groups and individuals bringing gifts including prophecy (Acts 19:6, 21:10–11); and there were clearly times when God was more present and active than at others, even during the ministry of Jesus himself (compare Mark 6:5 with Luke 5:17).

The primitive church clearly had both a theology and

experience of God 'coming'. In Acts 4:31 the building itself shakes as God comes to equip his people in response to their prayer and in chapter 10 verse 44 God interrupts Peter's sermon by coming upon the people in Cornelius' house. This expectation continued in the church, and as liturgies began to be written down, a part known as the '*epiclesis*' appeared, first of all in the Eucharistic prayer of Hippolytus, from the third century. This was the 'calling down' of the Holy Spirit by the celebrant of Communion on both the elements and also on the congregation. The prominence of the epiclesis has varied in different prayers down the centuries (it is to all intents and purposes absent from the 1662 Prayer Book) but in the Third Eucharistic Prayer of the ASB it is reinstated clearly and explicitly: 'Send the Holy Spirit on your people...' The same expectation, of God coming by his Spirit, is evident in the Anglican Confirmation service, where the bishop stretches out his hands towards the candidates and prays: 'Let your Holy Spirit rest upon them...'

It is not just in the liturgical tradition, though, that a theology of God 'coming' upon his people may be found. It is equally evident in hymnody. Even the most cursory glance through the 'Holy Spirit' section of a hymn book will prove this. Such words as 'Come, gracious Spirit, heavenly Dove', 'Come down O Love divine', 'Descend, O heavenly Dove', 'Descend with all thy gracious powers, O come, great Spirit, come' and many others suggest that Christians down the centuries have had a theology which allows for the 'coming' of God by his Spirit, even if they may not quite have had some of the experiences evidenced in the early church and now being restored by God in this charismatic era. All the evidence from Scripture, liturgy, hymnody and of course personal experience led me to the point where I couldn't help but conclude that God does come among his people at special times in a way in which he is not normally manifest.

But how are we to understand this? How can we talk of the 'presence' of God in worship when it is a fundamental belief of Christians that God is omnipresent? What meaning has the practice, so common in the ministry of people such as John Wimber, of 'inviting God to come', when we believe his presence pervades the universe at all times?

The problem arises, it seems to me, if we think in terms of only two possible categories, 'presence' or 'absence'. However, we know from all sorts of experience that there may be different types of presence. The experience of Christians does not always go along on a completely even keel: we speak about times of greater awareness of the presence of God, or of times when we felt especially 'close' to God. These different types of presence can be helpfully illustrated in terms of 'intensity' and 'relationship'.

Picture a piece of newspaper lying in the sun on a hot day. The sun's rays are warming it, but only if an ingenious Boy Scout comes along with a magnifying glass and holds it a few inches away will it begin to smoulder and eventually catch fire. The sun was not 'absent' before this point, but now its energy has been focused and intensified. It is a common experience to feel oneself for a time the special focus of God's attention and concern without suggesting that at other times he is not there or not interested in us personally.

Imagine, secondly, a visit to the theatre or cinema. In occupying our seat we may be no more than a few inches away from another person, perhaps even touching them at times. Yet at the end of the show we leave the theatre having had no real contact and no relationship whatsoever with the one to whom we were so physically close. They were there all right, but their presence had absolutely no impact on us at all. So it is with God: his omnipresence may have no actual value for those with whom he is present if there is no contact or relationship.

These two illustrations provide ways in which we might

appropriately speak of God's 'presence' in worship, while not denying it at other times, and thus an 'inviting' of the Holy Spirit is not a summoning up of an otherwise absent God, but rather a call for him to intensify his presence such that we are drawn into conscious awareness of relationship with him and action by him. A prayer from the Russian Orthodox tradition which functions in the same way as the Anglican 'Collect for Purity' celebrates beautifully both the omnipresence of the Spirit and our need of his presence as we worship:

> O Heavenly King, the Comforter, the Spirit of truth, who art in all places and fillest all things, the treasure of blessings and the giver of life, descend and rest upon us, and cleanse us from all impurity, and save our souls, O gracious God.[2]

So it is not theologically or practically incorrect to speak of God coming. However, I have recently begun to question whether it is the *best* way to describe what we experience as we worship. I'm concerned, first of all, about the times when there are not bodies littering the floor. If we talk positively about God's presence, it is quite difficult to avoid at such times at least thinking (even if we don't actually say anything) about his absence. Secondly, I would want to do everything I could to prevent Christians moving away from an understanding of worship as us entering humbly into God's presence: that is a great temptation when we think we can summon him into ours. He is not at our beck and call, and I've grown increasingly unhappy with language, however much we use it as shorthand for the initiated, which seems to suggest that he is.

But more importantly, I think we need to rediscover what it means to have a trinitarian understanding of worship. I do not mean by that that we need to make sure that all three of them get an equal amount of attention, but rather that the dynamic life and relationships of Father, Son and Spirit are reflected in the ways we talk about worship. Let me explain what I mean.

Around AD 318 a priest from Alexandria named Arius began to champion the belief that Jesus Christ was not really God, but was merely a created being. Although God graciously called him his son, he did not share the divine nature, had not always existed, and did not know and could therefore not reveal God fully. Arianism, as this heresy was called after its propagator, was finally defeated and outlawed by the Council of Nicaea in 325. While this was a blow for orthodoxy against heresy, it did not leave the church unscarred. The Council left Christians very reluctant to talk about the human Jesus, lest they should be opening themselves to the charge of heresy.

Yet the fact is that Jesus was, *and still is*, fully human. The letter to the Hebrews explains that no earthly priest was able to bring the right sort of worship to God because of his own sin, but that Jesus, in his sinless perfection, took on the role of priest to offer worship for us:

> For this reason he had to be made like his brothers and sisters in every way, in order that he might become a merciful and faithful high priest in service to God, and that he might make atonement for the sins of the people (Heb 2:17).

> The point of what we are saying is this: We do have such a high priest, who sat down at the right hand of the throne of the Majesty in heaven, and who serves in the sanctuary, the true tabernacle set up by the Lord, not by man (Heb 8:1-2).

The Greek word for the one who 'serves' or ministers in the second passage is *leitourgos*, the word from which we get 'liturgy'. To put it in modern terminology, the author is saying that Jesus is our 'Worship Leader': like Graham Kendrick or Matt Redman he stands up in front of the congregation and leads us into God's presence.

Theologian Alasdair Heron suggests that this is a part of

the ministry of Jesus which has largely been forgotten by the church down the years. If we don't quite dare talk of him as fully human he hasn't actually been made like us in every way, so we've needed to fill the gap with other holy but human figures such as Mary and the other saints. And if Jesus is fully divine without being fully human he becomes the object, rather than the offerer, of our worship. Heron explains:

> We worship, the *church* worships, and he is the object of worship rather than its leader… the church becomes in effect a substitute for Christ, and we are thrown back on our own pitifully inadequate resources in attempting to worship God.[3]

James Torrance takes this thinking even further in a very important book which all Christians should read.[4] He distinguishes between unitarian worship, which we offer to God from our human resources, and trinitarian worship, which is our participation in the worship offered to the Father by Jesus in the context of the Trinity. The role of the Holy Spirit, just to complete the picture, is to draw us into the mutual love and worship of the persons of the Trinity.

One immediate and very liberating implication of all this is that *worship is not up to us*. There can be so much pressure around, especially in charismatic churches, to perform, to do the right things and to feel the right things. If we don't, we must simply try harder. But when Graham, Noel or Matt are up there on the platform in front of us, a huge weight falls from our shoulders: it's their job, not ours, to get it right. We can simply enjoy what they're doing and join in as far as we can. We may at times get really caught up in it, become lost in wonder, love and praise; at other times we may feel less involved. But worship is being offered, and that is what's important: whether we're flitting around the edges or right there in the centre doesn't seem to matter quite so much.

In the same way, having Jesus as our worship leader is liberating: he will be offering perfect worship to the Father and all we have to do is allow ourselves to get caught up into it. If for some reason we are having a really off day, it doesn't matter, at least on one level. It isn't up to us to make it happen, it's the responsibility of our heavenly *leitourgos*.

But what has all this got to do with the Spirit coming or not? Quite simply, I believe that it is more helpful to see the work of the Spirit in terms of catching us up to where God is than bringing God down to where we are. Immediately we say that, of course, we run into problems because worship is not physically spatial in the way that statement implies. In one sense God is not 'up' while we are 'down', but the point remains: a trinitarian understanding of worship is more about us being carried into God's presence than him being called into ours.

This new understanding of trinitarian worship has made me modify my language, even if the end results are almost identical. There are still times when our worship feels as if it has touched heaven and other times when it feels as if it has hit rock bottom! But instead of asking myself 'Did God turn up?' I now prefer to ask 'Did we meet with God?'; not 'Did the Spirit come?' but 'Did the Spirit catch us up into the presence of the Father and the Son?' I am more and more convinced that the language of 'meeting' and 'encounter' is a much more helpful and theologically accurate way of describing worship than talking about whether or not God has shown up.

Charismatics have always had great expectations when it comes to worship. John Goldingay, reflecting on this fact, comments that

> charismatic spirituality assumes that it is normal on a continuing basis for the church and for the individual believer to have a felt sense of the presence and power of God, and a felt joy in God or enthusiasm about God.[5]

In one sense it doesn't matter where or how we have met with God, whether it takes place at his place or ours, as long as we do meet. But theology does matter, and while 'coming' language and 'being caught up' language are both biblical, I'm increasingly feeling far more happy with the latter, and the trinitarian understanding of worship behind it.

So what might happen when we do meet up? Of course God enjoys it, just as anyone enjoys quality time with those they love deeply and passionately. We are drawn into the joy and peace of his Spirit and into renewed relationship with him, both individually and corporately, and as an added bonus those outside that relationship begin to get a glimpse of what it is that they are missing. Truth may be proclaimed and learned as we worship, and the deeper we get into our worship, the more real becomes God's presence with us and ours with him.

This intimacy is the thing we desire most of all, of course, but when we are that close to him God begins to act among us, and we may experience some lovely side-effects. I want to look at these in some detail, since they are less easily understood and, I regret to say, more rarely actually experienced. However, my conviction is that since God is God, he is likely to do the same sort of things whenever we deliberately spend time with him. In other words, we ought to expect similar things to happen as happened when he spent time among us once before in his Son Jesus. From my experience so far, I've classified five of them, but that's not to say that there might not be more.

1. Warfare

I can't claim to understand this fully, but I believe that when we worship in spirit and in truth we engage in spiritual warfare with Satan and his minions. It's certainly true on an individual level that during worship people in some way affected by demonic forces are often brought to the point of release. It's not that uncommon during a worship time suddenly to hear screams and shrieks from someone in the congregation, even when we're not singing at that point, as a demon is forced to manifest itself. I think the example of the demonised man in Mark 1:21 ff illustrates this well. The Good News Bible translates verse 23 as meaning that the man 'came into the synagogue', leaving one with the impression that he was some weirdo who simply happened to wander in off the street. However, there's nothing in the Greek to suggest that this is the case. It's far more likely that he was already in there, an ordinary member of the congregation quite unaware of any problem – until Jesus arrives. He may even have been a synagogue-warden, if they had them then. Probably no one was more surprised than he was at his outburst. It wasn't as if he did it a lot. But when Jesus came into town, all sorts of hidden darkness was revealed and forced to manifest itself. The same happens in worship nowadays from time to time, and the common factor in both cases is simply that God is close in a way different from usual.

But I believe that there is more to worship than warfare against demonic forces which influence individuals. There is power in worship which works on a larger scale against the enemies of God in the spiritual realm. When we declare God's praises in worship, we are engaging in what Peter Wagner calls 'Strategic-level Spiritual Warfare' and witnessing to the principalities and powers which affect various areas and realms of society that they are defeated, that their power is cut off, and that before the name of Jesus through whom we worship and who is in fact enthroned on our praises and present with us, they must fall in cringing terror.[6] This is the theology behind 'praise marches', like Graham Kendrick's *Make Way!* and its many successors, where the church invades areas where Satan has much authority and proclaims his defeat in worship.

2. Healing

The second side-effect is that people are healed both physically and emotionally during worship. Healing formed a major part of the agenda of Jesus when he was physically on earth, and he loves to do the same today when he meets with us. I must admit that in my own experience this is nowhere near as common as I would like it to be, but I have known times when people have been spontaneously healed by the Lord while worshipping him. And on many other occasions the Spirit has come to rest upon individuals during worship so that those experienced in ministry can recognise God's touch on them and begin to pray for them. People may be touched on an emotional level too during worship, and receive some kind of healing or refreshment, or release from past hurts which are troubling them unconsciously.

3. Conviction

Jesus promised that the Holy Spirit, when he came, would convict of sin (Jn 16:8). He still does the same today, and it is during worship that he does it most frequently and most strongly. In a sense that is only to be expected, since a glimpse of the living God in all his holiness and glory is bound to make us feel a little diffident about our own achievements in the righteousness stakes. Isaiah found this to be true when he saw his vision of God (Is 6:1–7). The more the cherubim declared him to be holy, the more Isaiah was made aware of his own profound uncleanness and that of the people with whom he shared his humanity. It was only the Lord, and that on his own initiative, who could deal with this state of terminal unrighteousness. So as we worship today and let God in close enough, as it were, to see the really mucky areas of our lives, he brings with him both the uncomfortable ability to spotlight just what it was that we were hoping to hide from him, and very often from ourselves, and the wonderful gift of free forgiveness through his Son's blood shed on the cross. In true worship we have no secrets from God; we withhold from him no area of our lives, however reluctantly we open up, and he withholds from us no measure of his cleansing and forgiving love.

4. Conversion

When the process described above takes place in the life of a Christian, it is like a cleaning out of the spiritual system, and is usually quite undramatic; a transaction that goes on in the mind and heart between the individual and God. At times, of course, quite a struggle may go on, for example if there is an area of sin which is deeply ingrained and over which the person has been arguing with God and their conscience for some time, but normally this is a fairly routine matter, not unlike the daily confession of sins secretly to God in prayer. But when non-Christians find themselves under the same conviction, conversion is usually the result. This is the way in which the revivals of the past have worked; God seems suddenly to come upon an area and begins to break people's hearts wide open; first the believers, causing them to repent of backsliding and spiritual lethargy, and then on the community in general. My favourite account of this phenomenon concerns the Hebridean revival of 1949. Duncan Campbell of the Faith Mission went to preach in the town of Barvas, near Stornoway. After the service, about thirty or so people went to a nearby cottage to pray:

'God was beginning to move, the heavens were opening, we were there on our faces before God. Three o'clock in the morning came, and GOD SWEPT IN. About a dozen men and women lay prostrate on the floor, speechless. Something had happened; we knew that the forces of darkness were going to be driven back, and men were going to be delivered. We left the cottage at 3 a.m. to discover men and women seeking God. I walked along a country road, and found three men on their faces, crying to God for mercy. There was a light in every home, no-one seemed to think of sleep.'

When Duncan and his friends gathered at the church later in the morning, the place was crowded. A stream of buses came from every part of the island, yet no-one could discover who had told them to come. A butcher in his van had brought seven men from a distance of seventeen miles: all seven were gloriously converted. Now the revival was really under way. The Spirit of God was at work. All over the church men and women were crying for mercy. Some fell into a trance, some swooned, many wept.

Campbell pronounced the benediction and almost all left the chapel. Suddenly a young man began to pray. He was so burdened for the souls of his friends that he prayed for almost three-quarters of an hour. During this time the people returned to the church, joined by many others, until there were twice as many outside as inside. In some amazing way the people gathered from Stornoway, and Ness and different parishes. It was 4 a.m. the following morning before Duncan pronounced the benediction for a second time.

Even then he was still unable to go home to bed. As he was leaving the church a messenger told him, 'Mr. Campbell, people are gathered at the police station, from the other end of the parish; they are in great spiritual distress. Can anyone here come along and pray with them?' Campbell went and what a sight met him. Under the still starlit sky he found men and women on the road, others by the side of a cottage, and some behind a peat stack – all crying to God for mercy. The revival had come.

That went on for five weeks with services from early morning until late at night – or into the early hours of the morning. Then it spread to the neighbouring parishes. What had happened in Barvas was repeated over and over again.[7]

Conversion, as well as the dramatic conviction of lukewarm believers, seems to have been a major hallmark of John Wesley's ministry in eighteenth-century Britain. In his Journal are many accounts of the direct action of the Spirit during services of worship and preaching. In July 1762 he received this letter from Ireland, where he had recently been preaching:

> There is a glorious work going on at Limerick. Twelve or fourteen have a clear sense of being renewed; several have been justified this week; and on Sunday night there was such a cry as I scarce ever heard before, such confession of sins, such pleading with the Lord, and such a spirit of prayer as if the Lord himself had been visibly present among us. Some received remission of sins, and several were just brought to the birth. All were in floods of tears; they trembled, they cried, they prayed, they roared aloud, all of them lying on the ground. I began to sing, yet they could not rise, but sang as they lay along. Some of them stayed in the house all night; and, blessed be our God, they all hitherto walk worthy of their calling.[8]

Ten years later, in June 1772, the same phenomena were still continuing under Wesley's ministry, although he does seem to have had a knack of missing the best bits himself. Another letter describes a memorable evening in Weardale just after he had left for Sunderland:

> On Saturday evening God was present through the whole service, but especially toward the conclusion. Then one and another dropped down, till six lay on the ground together roaring for the disquietude of their hearts. Observing many to be quite amazed at this, I besought them to stand still and see the salvation of God, but the cry of the distressed soon drowned my voice. So I dismissed the congregation. About half of them went away. I continued praying with the rest when my voice could be heard; when it could not I prayed without a voice, till after ten o'clock. In this time, four of those poor mourners were clothed with the robes of praise.[9]

However, Wesley was to have some fun of his own the next night in Sunderland:

> In the evening we mightily wrestled with God for an enlargement of his work. As we were concluding, an eminent backslider came strongly into my mind; and I broke out abruptly, 'Lord, is Saul also among the prophets? Is James Watson here? If he be, show thy power!' Down dropped James Watson like a stone, and began crying aloud for mercy.[10]

This process is not, however, limited to times past. Although we still await revival of that sort in our day in England, there is a feeling everywhere in the air that we may not have to wait much longer, and we are beginning to see glimpses of such phenomena. Under the ministry of John Wimber we have been introduced to the concept of 'power evangelism', where people are convicted and brought to faith by the direct working of the Spirit in some supernatural way, rather than by becoming convinced of the truth of the gospel by intellectual argument. Often this takes place in the context of worship, where people sense the presence of something the like of which they've never come across before, and also a change in themselves while being totally unable to articulate in precise Christian jargon exactly what has happened. Obviously there is then the need to explain the theology and to see if they still like it, but generally most people do!

A young couple turned up out of the blue to a church service in which I was involved. They weren't churchgoers, but had been to a funeral during the week where the song 'Majesty' had been used, and something had got to them in such a way that they felt the need to pay a proper visit to church. I chatted briefly to them after the service, and thought nothing more of it until 11.30 the same evening when there was a knock on the door and I found the two of them on the doorstep in a state of great agitation. They had been fine, if slightly bored, in the service until we began to sing (not that stunning a worship slot, by my estimation), at which point the pair of them began, without any warning at all, to shake and quiver. The service eventually ended, but the shaking, unfortunately, did not. They had headed for the nearest pub, thinking that a couple of drinks would straighten them out, but they only ended up sitting in a pool of slopped beer. Eventually, still wobbling, they had come in desperation to see me.

'What's happening to us?' they wanted to know. Having been handed that one on a plate by the Spirit, I quickly and simply explained that God was touching them, that he had a claim on their lives to which they needed to respond, and that they could do so now. We went through *Journey into Life* together, and they went on their way rejoicing but no longer vibrating. Such spontaneous conversions will, I believe, become more and more common as the church increasingly rediscovers the power of the present Christ in worship. Obviously it doesn't do away with the need for personal evangelism and witness, or to be able to give a good account of what and why we believe, or to lead people to an intellectual understanding of, and a decision of the will to embrace the gospel, but it certainly does make the task of evangelism easier.

It needs to be said, of course, that not every strange manifestation which may take place during worship is to be welcomed as a manifestation of the Holy Spirit. The Bible is clear on the need to test the spirits and to discern the difference between divine, human and demonic manifestations. I'll say more about this later, but one of the most important tests involves looking for the fruit which is produced. It appears that churches which go in for 'power evangelism' seem to have a pretty good record in this area. If God chooses genuinely to bring people into the kingdom in ways which seem strange, we do well to get used to it.

One thing which I believe affects the fruit of a so-called

conversion is the degree to which conviction has been a part of the process. People tend to see their conversion (if they understand what has happened in terms of 'conversion' at all) in one of two ways, which I often refer to as a 'Mars Bar' conversion or a 'Lifebelt' conversion. If someone were to come up to me and very graciously give me a Mars Bar I would, of course, be grateful. Their generosity would make me think more of them, and if I had a chance I would try to repay their gift. But if I were drowning rather than just hungry, and someone threw me a lifebelt, I would be a bit more than grateful. I would be for ever in their debt; I would literally owe them my life, and nothing I could do or say could ever repay or even express what they had done for me.

Many Christians regard Jesus as nothing more than a purveyor of Mars Bars. Their life was going pretty well, but Jesus came along and gave them something nice which made it even better. Now they quite like him, and they may even feel they'd like to do him a good turn now and again to show that they were pleased. But others came to faith in a crisis: for some reason or other they were desperate, and were so consumed by their own guilt and the mess it was causing them and others that they cried out to Jesus for their life. When they experienced his forgiveness, nothing was ever the same again, and nothing was too much trouble to show their hearts' gratitude.

I believe that one reason why the church is so full of people who lack commitment, passion, evangelistic zeal (and who won't give financially) is that they have never really been broken down before God to the point that they literally cried out to him for mercy. They don't regard themselves as wicked sinners snatched by nothing but God's grace from the jaws of hell; they're simply nice people to whom Jesus has given a bit more peace or purpose or something. It is a well-known fact that it is possible for things to go wrong during the birth process of a baby, so that some kind of residual disability is present throughout life. In the same way Christians who had a defective birth are likely to remain handicapped for the rest of their Christian lives, unless they can be broken before God and 'born again' properly. It seems to be a characteristic of revival that those who are converted arrive in the kingdom via a lifebelt, as the accounts quoted above show.

We've seen many people come to faith in the churches I've served in over the years, but I'll never forget one carol service when I was approached by a woman with tears streaming down her face. She was on the outermost fringes of the church, but something in the service had got to her, and as we sat in the vestry afterwards she told me about the mess her life was in due to a major fraud in which she had been involved. How could she ever find forgiveness? I told her, and before long her tears had turned to tears of joy and relief. Her growth in discipleship since then has been phenomenal, and she is now in major leadership in that church. Some time later she asked me why it is that some new Christians seem to stay where they are in terms of commitment while others, like her, seem to be on a kind of spiritual 'fast-track'. I'm sure the answer has a tremendous amount to do with the nature of their Christian birth, and the degree of brokenness it involved. Just imagine a church made up entirely of people who feel and know that they owe Jesus absolutely everything, who have a passionate hatred of even a hint of sin or compromise, and whose hearts' desire is to see others brought to know this Jesus! There'd be no stopping us!

5. Empowering

As it is the work of the Spirit to convict us of sin, so also it is his task to empower us for service. Worship is an ideal context for this to happen, as we open ourselves up to God for a fresh vision of his glory and offer ourselves once again in love and service to him. Many people experience the filling or baptism of the Spirit for the first time during worship, and especially during times of singing in tongues; others simply receive a new influx of power or boldness, or a fresh vision of some area of ministry. Returning to Isaiah's vision, we can see that after receiving cleansing from God he was then equipped by being given the prophetic task and message (Is 6:8–13).

Many of the manifestations of the 'Toronto blessing' seem to have this character about them. Those who prefer to call it 'The Refreshing' have cottoned on to an important emphasis which the Spirit seems to be placing before us as, many believe, he prepares the church for worldwide revival, refreshing and renewing our love for God, his word, and those who are lost. Why it should take such dramatic manifestations to achieve this end I have no idea, and I certainly wouldn't want to try to explain what different manifestations mean, or even how many of them are genuinely from God and not just learned human behaviour. But I have no doubt that God is up to something, and what results I do see point to an equipping and anointing move of the Spirit.

So it is as we worship that we can often expect to be given a fresh anointing for whatever it is that God has for us to do in his kingdom. This will commonly come through the prophetic word as messages are given which not only call the church but which also empower it to obey the calling. That is one reason why spiritual gifts play such an important part in worship.

These, then, are some of the side-effects of God's encountering his people as they worship. The sort of things that Jesus and his Spirit love to do, they love to do especially when they meet with us during worship. I'm not saying that all this happens every time – it certainly doesn't when I'm leading – but we should expect some of it to happen some of the time, and we should expect it to increase as we grow in our ability to worship in spirit and in truth. It is very exciting indeed to be involved in a service when the Spirit really begins to move, and people all around are being touched in all sorts of ways. But we must never forget that these manifestations of the presence of God are only side-effects, marvellous though they are. The real point is that God himself is with us. That ought to be enough, though it is in the nature of God to do things for us and to us whenever he can get close enough. But if nothing at all happened, it would still be sufficient that the living God, Maker of heaven and earth, had come for a while to meet with his people and be enthroned on their praises.

Wonderful all this may be, but it perhaps seems a million miles away from the idea of 'liturgy' and the pictures it conjures up for us. So let's move on to ask some questions about what liturgy actually is, and why it is so important.

Notes

1 John Leach, *Liturgy and Liberty* (Eastbourne: MARC, 1989) pp 21–51.
2 Taken from the Liturgy of St John Chrysostom. See *The Orthodox Liturgy* (London: SPCK [for the Fellowship of SS Alban and Sergius], 1968) p 16
3 Alasdair Heron, *Table and Tradition* (Edinburgh: Handsel, 1983) p 82.
4 James B. Torrance, *Worship, Community, and the Triune God of Grace* (Carlisle: Paternoster, 1996).
5 John Goldingay, 'Charismatic Spirituality – some Theological Reflections' in *Theology 99* (1996) pp 178–187.
6 See Peter Wagner's *Confronting the Powers* (Ventura, Ca.: Regal, 1996) for an account of this subject.
7 Colin Whittaker, *Great Revivals* (Basingstoke: Marshall, Morgan and Scott, 1984), pp 159 ff.
8 John Wesley, *The Works of John Wesley*, Vol 3 (Grand Rapids,

MI: Zondervan, 1958–9), p 106.

9 *Ibid* p 470.

10 *Ibid* p 473.

2

Why Liturgy?

The lecture had, although I say it myself, gone rather well. They'd laughed in the right places, not laughed in the wrong places, nodded enthusiastically as I made my series of logical points which led inexorably to the inevitable conclusion that liturgy was absolutely essential for successful worship. At the end of the session people had spoken warmly to me, bought my books (the real test of success, of course) and generally been nice. But then one young man approached me, his face looking troubled. 'That was brilliant,' he said, much to my relief, 'but I do have one question. What *is* "liturgy"?' He'd fairly recently come to faith, he told me, in a New Church environment, and, while finding himself thoroughly convinced by my arguments about all the powerful properties of this commodity called 'liturgy' to enhance worship, bless people, keep the church sane and generally make everyone's shirts whiter, he had not the faintest idea what I had actually been talking about.

That is why I want to introduce the subject now, before going on in the next chapter to give all the reasons why I believe liturgy is so important, and especially so for those in what we might term 'renewed' or 'charismatic' churches. After that the rest of the book will provide a kind of 'how to' guide for those who find themselves leading, or being led in worship. So, what is liturgy?

Let's begin to answer that question with another one. What is 'happiness'? We all know it when we experience it, but defining it is much harder. To a new bride it might be togetherness with her husband; to a hiker on a hot day it might be a pint of lager. To a psychologist it might be an emotional response to an outside stimulus and the meaning associated with it which causes pleasure, and to a bio-chemist it would be the release of certain chemicals in the brain. But to you and me when our team scores a goal or our new baby is born healthy, these definitions by theorists and even by other ordinary people are irrelevant. Like art, we may not understand it but we know what we like.

We could attack the question 'What is liturgy?' in all sorts of ways. Theologians, anthropologists, sociologists and many others could all have a go, but at the end of the day we might not be any the wiser. All we know is that it's using a book in church. As a crude but reliable generalisation, the church in Britain can be divided neatly down the middle between those who like to use prayers and other words from a book, and those who like to make things up as they go along.

Sadly, there is often a certain amount of antagonism between these two camps, and in fact the tension between liturgy and liberty is not a new one. It has been a problem to some degree throughout most of the history of the church, and it can, I believe, be detected in the Bible itself, even in the Old Testament. Throughout much of the history of Israel two distinct strands of spirituality coexisted, often uneasily, side by side. The 'prophetic' strand was marked by a 'charismatic' style, an immediacy in experience of God, many 'signs and wonders', a great emphasis on personal holiness, and very often a suspicion of those who were more structured in their spirituality and who were therefore prone to nominalism. Prophets leave us with the impression that they were often rather hairy, unpredictable people who did all sorts of weird and ecstatic things.

On the other hand, the priests were the height of respectability. They went in for liturgy in vast quantities and on vast scales, and seemed at least for most of the time to have little respect for their unsavoury prophetic brothers-in-Yahweh. They were heavily into bureaucracy (as even the most cursory reading of the priestly writings, Chronicles, Ezra and Nehemiah reveals), and liked things to be done properly and according to tradition, with careful planning and clearly defined jobs for all. To be a priest was to be someone important in society, and the dignity of their calling was enhanced by their fine vestments.

Now, apart from the 'hairy' bit, if that isn't a description of the New Churches and the Church of England, I don't know what is! The liturgical 'establishment' types can regard their more spontaneous brothers and sisters as naive and theologically shallow, while secretly feeling terrified at the very thought of doing anything in worship without a book to prompt them; conversely those who love to meet God on the hoof can regard others as worshipping in the very ways the Bible warns about: formalism, dead works and vain repetition. In spite of the growing awareness of the need for spontaneity in liturgy and the growing interest in liturgy for the spontaneous, the gulf is still there and is, I suspect, much more of an emotional phenomenon than a theological one.

Yet it seems to me that in fact neither side has a monopoly on truth, and that both sides are prone to their own particular dangers. Yes, the priests could and in fact often did propagate nominal, meaningless worship, and yes, those interminable lists of names are pretty boring. But at the same time prophets could go off the rails too, and prophesy what they or their audiences wanted to hear. Jesus flatly refused to be identified totally with one strand or the other, and worked within the best of both traditions. If we in his church are to follow him properly, we cannot afford to ditch half of his spirituality, whether that half consists of healing the sick or taking part in liturgical worship.

So maybe we do after all need the help of some experts in understanding liturgy, and in particular where it came from, so that we can assess more objectively whether or not it is a Good Thing, even if we feel we don't like it. Let's begin our explanation with a story:

Once upon a time there were some people who worshipped a god. They had thought long and hard about how they should worship him, and in the end worked out a very careful method. They had special people called 'priests' who did bits of it for them, they had special buildings in which to do it, and they had exactly the right ways of cutting up and burning the animals which they thought their god liked to watch. And so for years and years, day in day out, they offered him worship like that.

One day a stranger wandered into town. He claimed to be a prophet who had been sent by the god to tell people what he *really* wanted them to do. From now on, said the prophet, you are all special priests, you don't need special places, and you certainly don't need that animal stuff. The god will give you all his special power so that you can worship him exactly as he wants any time, any place, anywhere.

Once they got used to the idea the people loved it. They realised that they had been just a bit bored with the former ways of doing things, and somewhat restricted in what they could say or do for the god. But now they were free: they could sing, dance, pray and praise to their little hearts' content. Nothing was ever the same twice running, and they just *knew* that the god loved it too.

But gradually the leaders began to get worried. They were a bit frightened of the freedom the people now had, and they really didn't like some of the outrageous things they sometimes got up to. And they weren't sure the god did either. So they began to make Rules, to stop the people from enjoying themselves so much, and to keep things in order. So that people would know what the Rules were, they wrote them down, and told people that the god only wanted to be worshipped by the Book. Before long the people only ever used the Book, and all the different things they did had disappeared. They started to have special people called 'priests' to do bits of it for them, they built special buildings in which to do it, and they had exactly the right ways of praying and praising (although they skipped the animals this time).

This fantasy story isn't so much of a fantasy for many people: it describes exactly their perception of the way in which Christians, having been freed from the rules and regulations of Old Testament religion and worship, promptly constructed the whole thing all over again. Jesus came to abolish liturgy, they say, and here we are two thousand years later still trapped by it.

This view is perhaps best exemplified in a quotation from the 1970s by the late Arthur Wallis, one of the early pioneers of the house church movement:

> [Traditions] put a yoke on the neck of disciples, and especially on their corporate worship which produces bondage. Liturgies and fixed forms of service... militate against our being able to 'worship by the Spirit of God'. Liturgies, whether ancient or modern, written or unwritten, are a human device, to keep the wheels turning by doing what is customary, rather than exercising faith in the immediate presence and operation of the Spirit. Consequently they cover up the need for the return of the Spirit when he has departed, and they hinder faith for spontaneity and variety.[1]

It has to be said that there is some evidence in the Bible for this kind of understanding of liturgy as something which we create in order to save ourselves the embarrassment of having to talk to God face to face without a book in between us. While Jesus seemed happy to join in with the worship of the temple and the synagogue, he was not uncritical of it or its officials, as Matthew 23 demonstrates.

He was clearly about to inaugurate a whole new way of worshipping, with a completely different spirit about it. The Samaritan woman in John 4 wants to discuss the mechanics of worship: should we do it on this mountain or that one? But Jesus isn't interested in that question: he wants to talk about the inward things of the spirit, and about truth. Paul too speaks of inward, spiritual worship as replacing 'official' organised worship: the sacrifice offered by Christians is to be their whole, holy lives, not a goat or dove (Rom 12:1).

This tension between the worship Jesus came to teach and bring and the established ways of doing things erupted in violence and became literally a matter of life and death when Stephen's accusers said:

> This fellow never stops speaking against this holy place and against the law. For we have heard him say that this Jesus of Nazareth will destroy this place and change the customs Moses handed down to us (Acts 6:13–14).

In his defence, Stephen explained that

> it was Solomon who built the house for [God]. However, the Most High does not live in houses made by men. As the prophet says: 'Heaven is my throne, and the earth is my footstool. What kind of house will you build for me?' says the Lord. 'Or where will my resting place be?' (Acts 7:47–49)

Stephen died because he dared to proclaim that the old Israelite ways of worshipping had to cease and be replaced by a new, inward, personal and spiritual worship.

So those who see modern liturgical worship as a reversion to something from which Jesus supposedly set us free do have a point. If the worship of the New Testament church was anything like the picture we have of it from 1 Corinthians 14, it clearly had been set free from liturgy and set forms. The liberty of the Spirit was all that counted, yet so quickly did those early Christians rebuild all that Jesus had demolished. Why on earth did they do it?

This is a good question, and its answer is very complicated. To begin with we will have to journey forwards through time for fourteen centuries to Mainz in Germany where Johann Gutenberg first printed a book (the Bible, as it happens) on a moveable printing press. This event, which must have seemed like a fairly major breakthrough at the time, had consequences far beyond the wildest dreams of the mediaeval Germans: it began to change the whole way we deal with information and, yes, even with worship.

Before that, you see, information was passed down orally from generation to generation and from place to place. People created, told and remembered stories, and since books had to be hand-written and were therefore very expensive and fairly rare, they were used as a focus for what everyone knew already, since they had learned it from someone who told them. There was also a corporate dimension to life: stories belonged to communities, and they were enjoyed by people together in groups.

But with the printing press came cheap and readily available books. The whole nature of the way people processed information and knowledge changed, and books, rather than being the custodians of the real, oral tradition, began to replace it as purveyors of truth. Social changes meant also that the corporate dimension began to weaken, so the net result was that if there were things to learn and discover people shut themselves away and read about them rather than getting together to hear about them. We can't overestimate the revolution which printing brought about, but we might compare it to the more recent revolution which has given us the technology to communicate through floppy disks and down phone lines. The effects are likely to be about as far-reaching.

What has all this got to do with liturgy and worship? It simply explains that to ask why the New Testament Christians didn't use prayer books is like asking why they didn't travel around in cars: the technology available to them didn't allow it. They used what they did have: donkeys. In the same way they worshipped with what they did have: oral tradition. How do you use oral tradition to pass on and celebrate information? Through short, pithy, memorable statements and stories, which were repeated until everyone knew them by heart; in other words liturgy. It wasn't a matter of apostasy; it was a matter of technology.

There are still vestiges of this oral tradition around. The Ladybird and the Zebra editions of the story of *Goldilocks and the Three Bears* may vary considerably in some of the finer details of the story, but they, and every other edition, contain the fateful line 'Who's been sleeping in *my* porridge?' (or something like that). Every child in the land could tell you that line: it's pure liturgy. The worship of the early church must have worked in a similar way: around differing accounts of the life and teaching of Jesus and the apostles were short, pithy sayings which were the common property of the whole community. They are often preserved in the Bible: the really important point of a parable, for example, can be found in its last line, a kind of punch line which sums up the whole teaching in a phrase. Theologians call these phrases 'pronouncement sayings'. Some examples might be 'In the same way your Father in heaven is not willing that any of these little ones should be lost' (Mt 18:14), 'This is how my heavenly Father will treat each of you unless you forgive your brother from your heart' (Mt 18:35), 'This is how it will be with anyone who stores up things for himself but is not rich towards God' (Lk 12:21) and so on.

But is this worship? It may be easy to understand how in that culture they learned their theology from 'liturgical' sayings, but surely they didn't have to stick to them in worship? Again we may be in danger of asking a twentieth-century question of a first-century church. For the early Christians there was no such thing as 'doctrine' as a distinct subdivision of Christianity, to be studied by academics. If doctrinal truth was like a butterfly, you observed and enjoyed it flying free, not pinned to a board. Michael Vasey explains:

> The worship of the Christian church is an expression of... Spirit-given life. It is not merely a rationally constructed embodiment of Christian belief and commitment. Even less is it a public performance imposed by ecclesiastical authority. Reason, Christian doctrine and ecclesiastical authority all have their part to play but essentially Christian worship is the corporate expression of the church's new life in Christ. It is a spontaneous growing thing that is shaped by many different factors, but which has its origin in the Holy Spirit.[2]

To try to separate doctrine from worship is a twentieth-century neurosis, not a first-century principle.

So why isn't there any liturgy in the Bible? There is loads of it! Leaving aside the Old Testament, there are in the New many examples of liturgical forms. There are fixed exclamations, often in a foreign language ('Amen', 'Abba', 'Maranatha!'), doxologies and blessings (1 Tim 1:17; Rom 11:33–36), hymns (Eph 5:14; 1 Tim 3:16), creeds (Rom 10:9; 1 Cor 8:6; 15:3–5), gestures (1 Tim 2:8; 1 Cor 16:20; Acts 21:5), and annual festivals (1 Cor 16:8). All these, and many others, would have been part of the worship of the first Christians, and would have been known and repeated by the community. The New Church rhetoric which sees biblical worship as nothing but completely spontaneous and never the same twice is, quite simply, wrong.

However, there obviously was some development which got us to the point today where liturgy is often perceived as restrictive and quenching of the Spirit. The incredible versatility of the human mind to distort and twist truth which resulted in the church needing to defend orthodoxy against heresy had a dramatic effect on liturgy. Creeds, in particular, moved from being joyous expressions of the community's experience of God to becoming fences which circumscribed truth. If you couldn't join in and mean the words you were beyond the pale. They expanded as new and even more creative heresies abounded. When a fourth-century heretic taught that Christ's rule would one day end, the clause 'Whose kingdom shall have no end' was tacked on to the current creed. Thus liturgy took on a new role as guardian of the truth.

Another major change must have come about with the legalisation of the church under Constantine in the fourth century. When you were meeting informally for worship in one another's homes, living exuberance was probably more important than theological exactitude. But now that you worshipped in official buildings, and you may well have some professional theologians (if not the Emperor himself) in the congregation, you had to mind your theological 'p's and 'q's rather more, so further spontaneity and flexibility was lost. And of course the new technology of printing had the effect eventually of standardising things almost totally.

So if you don't think you like liturgy because it means doing exactly the same thing week after week from the same book, the earliest Christians would be right with you. But they would part company with you if you thought authentic worship was never the same twice, contained nothing in which the community could join together, and could never use set and recognisable forms.

What is the state of the art today? Some churches quite deliberately use set liturgies: I am most familiar with the Anglican Church, but there are others. As far as the Church of England is concerned, we have recently emerged from a long period of fairly static liturgical form. The 1662 *Book of*

Common Prayer ruled supreme over most of the church for centuries; it almost successfully fought off a challenge in 1928; and only really in the 1970s did major change begin to erupt. After a decade of experimentation and a host of temporary texts, the *Alternative Service Book* (or the ASB) was published in 1980, the most radical thing to have happened liturgically for three hundred years. Yet it is almost true to say that the changes since then have been even more radical still. I believe charismatic renewal has been an important factor in those changes, although of course cultural and social changes have had a dramatic effect too.

One significant change has been the death of the concept of 'duty'. The Anglican liturgy itself tells us that worship is both a 'duty and a joy'. My parents' generation had a highly developed sense of duty: they must have had to put up for so long with worship which was so culturally outdated and in such foreign language and thought-forms. But my children's generation has almost totally lost any sense of duty: if it isn't a joy they simply won't bother with it. Worship must be alive and relevant if it is to attract people who live with constant and rapidly accelerating change and innovation. Worshippers nowadays expect to *feel* something as they meet with God, otherwise it simply isn't real to them. However we may decry this loss of 'duty' (and I certainly do), it is a fact with which we have to come to terms.

Thus there has been a move, even since 1980, away from set texts to hordes of alternatives; away from a wodge of unchangeable material towards a framework into which different and appropriate texts may be slotted. The technological developments of word-processing and desk-top publishing are beginning to have an effect on liturgy every bit as radical as the printing press did five-and-a-half centuries ago. And the advent of 'touchy-feely' charismatic worship has placed an expectation in the hearts of worshippers that some degree of joy (and emotion generally) should be a part of the whole experience of worship. Anthropologists have said (although, I note with interest, with some degree of hindsight) that experiences of unbridled emotion such as the 'Toronto blessing' has produced were the inevitable next stage of liturgical emancipation for Christians.

Liturgy, always shaped to a high degree by the culture and technology surrounding it, has come a long way to meet renewal. It is easy for those uncomfortable within a particular world to caricature it and then reject it, particularly if they have found a living faith in spite of, rather than because of, churches' practices. But as you'll see as you progress through this book, the sort of liturgy which I'm endeavouring to sell you is not the dead formalism of Elizabethan England but the new, creative worship being designed by liturgists and scholars for the next millennium. The New Churches and the Church of England have moved a long way towards each other, and not just in the way they worship; some liturgists seem genuinely to be interested in this movement (I have actually helped a Liturgical Commission member who wanted to write some 'Wimber-friendly' texts!), and this book is an attempt to bridge that gap even more.

So if, like my friend from the conference, you're not really sure what liturgy is, I hope this book will help. I hope you can forget some of the more negative impressions and caricatures you may have picked up and gain from the material here a more positive understanding. There are a lot of signs that within charismatic renewal the word 'liturgy' is about to become a buzz-word. I hope you enjoy and value my contribution to help this process, and having explained what I think liturgy is, I'll now attempt to convince you that it is essential!

Notes

1 Arthur Wallis, *The Radical Christian* (Eastbourne: Kingsway, 1981) pp 119f.
2 Michael Vasey in *Anglican Worship Today* (London: Collins, 1980) p 38.

3

Liturgy and Renewal

I don't want you to misunderstand this chapter. I must begin by saying what a tremendous debt I personally and the church generally owe to what has been called the 'house church' movement (now more usually known as the 'New Churches'). I am profoundly grateful to God that at a point when the established churches were in many ways at a very low ebb he raised up new and Spirit-filled congregations to breathe new life back into the church, and I am grateful for the many ways in which I have benefited from what God has been doing in the New Churches. I need to acknowledge too that they themselves have seen an evolution in their thinking: some of the rebellious anger of the early days was inevitable as people became scandalised by the state of the church, as was the exaggeration and blindness to what was good and right. But most of the New Churches haven't stayed there, and their openness to those in the mainstream who are seeking the same kind of renewal and spiritual life as they are has resulted in some deep heart-to-heart relationships and much benefit for all concerned. So I don't have a down on the New Churches, OK? It is not my intention to engage in any unseemly Anglican jingoism, and I apologise in advance for the times when I will appear to be doing just that.

However, I do want to continue my suggestion that it is just possible that one or two babies might have been thrown out with the bathwater. In particular I want to try to convince you (having explained to you what liturgy is) that our worship, and particularly worship which has a high value on openness to the Spirit, needs liturgy if it is to be balanced and well-rounded. I'll begin by examining three positions it is possible for a church to find itself in, and then give you twelve reasons why a correct understanding and use of liturgy might help.

So what might happen when charismatic renewal hits a church, particularly a liturgically minded church? In my experience we go into one of three modes.

Liturgical paralysis

This is the position of churches that would like in theory to be open to the Spirit, but sadly the book doesn't let them. People may have experienced personal renewal, and even renewal at a church level, but they are still seeking unsuccessfully to renew the worship of the church. How can the services and the liturgy actually be dragged into the charismatic era? The answer evades everyone, so the liturgy continues, and renewal, such as it is, is relegated to homegroups. Sunday services continue to be nothing more than a route march from page 119 to page 145, and woe betide anything which gets in the way.

Anglican restorationism

The other extreme occurs when churches have gone all out for renewal and in doing so have believed it necessary to abandon liturgy altogether. They have bought lock, stock and barrel all the early seventies house church rhetoric about liturgy being dead, formal, vain repetition (a view which, as we have already mentioned, most of the New

Churches don't believe any longer), and have thrown out the whole lot when it comes to liturgy. So an Anglican service becomes forty-five minutes of singing, a sermon, and then all fall down. Perhaps even worse, there may be others who go through the liturgical motions because they feel they have to, while longing for the part of the service when they get into the 'worship slot' and begin to do the 'real' worshipping. The need for churches in this group is not so much for a renewal of the liturgy as for a liturgising of the renewal.

Charismatic schizophrenia

Thirdly, and perhaps this is the largest group, there are those who fall in between these other two, and who feel as if they have renewal in one hand and liturgy in the other and don't know quite what to do with either of them. What tends to happen is that any overt activity of the Spirit is relegated to a slot after the service. We love and we welcome charismatic goings on, but we're just not sure where to fit them.

The clearest example of this that I can remember was one occasion when I was part of a mission team on a weekend in another parish. The weekend had gone well, the teaching had been received with enthusiasm, the musicians I had taken with me had done their job effectively, and we were looking forward to the final Sunday evening celebration which would round the whole thing off. However, there was one small problem: Evensong. Because of the rather elderly, conservative congregation normally present at the evening service, the vicar decided to play it straight, and then leave a five-minute gap for anyone who wanted to leave (the congregation, for example), before continuing with the celebration, when I would be set free to carry on with some of the more outrageous aspects of my ministry. Ever happy to oblige I agreed, and it did seem like the most loving and tactful way to handle the situation, but I couldn't help feeling that there was a kind of sad, ironic truth in the announcement the vicar made to the people at the beginning of Evensong that 'after the service has finished there will be a time of worship'.

This kind of attitude to liturgy is illustrated very well in two quotations, both commenting on the same biblical passage. Chapters 5–7 of 2 Chronicles deal with the dedication of the Temple in Jerusalem, and verses 12–14 of chapter 5 describe the high spot of the service:

> All the Levites who were musicians – Asaph, Heman, Jeduthun and their sons and relatives – stood on the east side of the altar, dressed in fine linen and playing cymbals, harps and lyres. They were accompanied by 120 priests sounding trumpets. The trumpeters and singers joined in unison, as with one voice, to give praise and thanks to the LORD. Accompanied by trumpets, cymbals and other instruments, they raised their voices in praise to the LORD and sang:
>
> 'He is good;
>   his love endures for ever.'
>
> Then the temple of the LORD was filled with a cloud, and the priests could not perform their service because of the cloud, for the glory of the LORD filled the temple of God.

My first quotation is from a book on worship written from a New Church background; a book which, in the circumstances, I won't identify:

> Sometimes, when we dare to let the Lord have his say, schedules and programmes have to be put away. 2 Chronicles 5:13–14 describes how when the glory of the Lord filled the house of God those who were 'booked' to minister laid aside their ministry. Can you imagine it? All the work was finished. The house of the Lord was prepared. Choirs were rehearsed, trumpets were polished, 'the band' was ready... the sermon for

the grand opening had been sweated over for months, and then somebody started a chorus: 'The Lord is good and his mercy endureth for ever'. It took off! The place resounded with their united thanksgiving, and God inhabited their praise. He joined them. His glory filled the house.

Be sure of this: when God really gets involved with the gathering of his people you may as well forget [what you've planned]. The King must do what the King must do!

Another way of looking at the same passage is expressed in my second quotation:

Note that here, as in many other places in the Old Testament, free exuberant worship does not exclude careful planning, preparation, direction and liturgy, but happens within a structured context. All is not lost for Anglicans after all!

Emotionally, some people will resonate much more with the former rather than the latter, and others vice versa. The problem is that the text simply does not bear the interpretation put on it in the first quote, while the second (which just happens to be from me) gives a much more accurate picture of what was going on. I am convinced that it was exactly that planning and preparation which facilitated the Lord's coming among his people, and this whole book is written from that passionate belief.

But why do we need liturgy at all? If the 2 Chronicles passage really does say that it helped on that occasion, that doesn't mean we have to put up with it every week. Maybe that was just a lucky fluke! After all, you only have to look at some of the liturgical churches to see that God appears to be notable by his absence. Haven't we charismatics outgrown such boring things now that we have received the outpouring of the Spirit and experienced his liberty in our worship? I want to give you twelve reasons why I believe such thinking can be erroneous and at times arrogant, and why renewal desperately needs the structuring which liturgy can provide.

1. Liturgy and roots

Our post-modern world has a strangely ambivalent attitude to history. On the one hand novelty is exciting, youth is to be worshipped and anything much older than about three weeks is ready for the scrap-heap, while on the other hand the whole of our past heritage is there to be quarried for useful things to add to our selection of pick-and-mix resources. We lack any sense of rootedness: the past does not really belong to us, and we do not really belong to it; it is just there to be picked up if we feel like it, as we might with Murray Mints or Coca-Cola-flavoured worms from the counter in Woolworths. Church history is often greeted with a huge yawn, while at the same time there is a great revival of interest in Celtic spirituality, and cutting-edge radical movements like the now sadly defunct Nine O'clock Service combine ambient electronic sounds with Latin chants and Eastern Orthodox ceremonial. Just what is history, and might it be good for us? And if so, how does liturgy help us to get in touch with it?

Clearly those of us involved in charismatic renewal are interested in new things. Many of us have rebelled (albeit in different ways) against the dead sterility of much that is past, the worship of tradition which puts it on a pedestal so high that we can't even dust it, let alone change it, and the Anglican motto 'As it was in the beginning is now and ever shall be, world without end. Amen.' We worship a God who makes all things new, and we rejoice to be alive in such exciting times when he seems to be on the move as never before. It is just a short step of logic to say that if new equals good, old equals bad, and it is a step which is very tempting to take.

One interesting example of this 'philosophy of history'

(or way of understanding it) is expressed graphically in Andrew Walker's critique of the house churches, *Restoring the Kingdom*. We have already noted that much New Church thinking and practice has evolved since the early days, and Walker has taken a still photograph of one particular period of their development. Nevertheless, the graph still reflects a popular view, not least among Anglican charismatics![1]

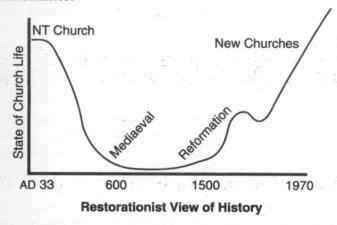

Restorationist View of History

In a nutshell, it reflects the idea that the New Testament standards of authentic Christianity began slowly to decline soon after the Bible account stops, and continued downhill until they reached rock-bottom in about AD 600. The next 900 years were spent in the bottom of the pits, until suddenly God's Spirit began to move through the Reformation and various evangelical renewal movements and things got better and better. Then along came the house churches: they were the latest move of the Spirit in which God was going to restore all things to their former glory and usher in the end of time.

Clearly this is a very biased (not to say grossly inaccurate) way of viewing history. It allows us to write off nearly everything from the past, since it is always the present which is the 'real thing'. So the spiritual riches of saints from Augustine to Thomas à Kempis are worthless, since their authors lived during the long period when nothing was happening. If we are part of a renewal movement it is easy for us to imbibe this thinking, and at a much quicker rate. Nowadays many worship songs are past it within a year at the most – it is always the latest which is the best. An appreciation of liturgy can help us not just to rediscover lost riches from the past, but to see ourselves in a continuity with them. The liturgy available to us now is the culmination of a long process stretching back for centuries. The church has been seeking the best ways to formulate its public worship down the years, and a tremendous amount of hard work and prayer has gone into the evolution of the liturgy we now use. The creativity of scholars and poets, some no doubt more and some less devout than others, the doctrinal sharpening up of truth by theologians, the discussions and disagreements which have been resolved into consensus: all these have left us the legacy through which we can now meet God in worship. To ignore this legacy is not only blindness, it is also dangerous. Any generation which thinks that it is self-sufficient and has no need to learn the lessons of the past or to rejoice thankfully in its inheritance is heading for trouble. And yet, sadly, it is all too common for us to undervalue the past. As someone once put it:

History repeats itself.
   Has to.
   No one listens.

'Anyone who refuses to learn from the mistakes of history,' said another writer, 'is doomed to repeat them.'

I went through a stage a while ago where the Lord began to speak to me about historical continuity. It suddenly struck me that when I used a psalm to express my feelings to God in a particular situation, I was using the same words which had been used by countless people down the centuries in many different, or even similar, situations. I already knew this, of course, but one day it really struck me in a way which went deeply into my heart and has affected the way I have prayed ever since. As I read, for example, Psalm 103, I really began to get in touch with others who may have used the same psalm in the past. I could picture myself joining with the Israelite community in the Temple in Jerusalem, being there as a young boy called Jesus learned the words with his father Joseph, attending a Mass celebrated by Thomas à Becket (my favourite historical character) in Canterbury Cathedral, and so on down the ages until I arrived in an urban parish in the Midlands at the end of the twentieth century, still using the same words. Our worship can be greatly enriched if we get in touch with other worshippers, both worldwide and down the ages, by sharing with them in the liturgy.

This continuity reaches its climax in that most central aspect of Christian worship, the Communion or Eucharist. In a beautiful and well-known passage in his book *The Shape of the Liturgy*, Gregory Dix, an Anglican Benedictine monk, describes the same experience I had when reading the Psalms. Commenting on Jesus' command to 'do this in remembrance of me', he asks:

Was ever another command so obeyed? For century after century, spreading slowly to every continent and country and among every race on earth, this action has been done, in every conceivable human circumstance, for every conceivable human need from infancy and before it to extreme old age and after it, from the pinnacles of earthly greatness to the refuge of fugitives in the caves and dens of the earth. Men have found no better thing than this to do for kings at their crowning and for criminals going to the scaffold; for armies' triumph or for a bride and bridegroom in a little country church; for the proclamation of a dogma or for a good crop of wheat; for the wisdom of a Parliament of a mighty nation or for a sick old

woman afraid to die; for a schoolboy sitting an examination or
for Columbus setting out to discover America; for the famine
of whole provinces or for the soul of a dead lover; in
thankfulness because my father did not die of pneumonia; for a
village headman much tempted to return to fetish because the
yams had failed; because the Turk was at the gates of Vienna;
for the repentance of Margaret; for the settlement of a strike;
for a son for a barren woman; for Captain so-and-so, wounded
and prisoner of war; while the lions roared in the nearby
amphitheatre; on the beach at Dunkirk; while the hiss of
scythes in the thick June grass came faintly through the
windows of the church; tremulously, by an old monk on the
fiftieth anniversary of his vows; furtively, by an exiled bishop
who had hewn timber all day in a prison camp near Murmansk;
gorgeously, for the canonization of S. Joan of Arc – one could
fill many pages with the reasons why men have done this, and
not tell a hundredth part of them. And best of all, week by
week and month by month, on a hundred thousand successive
Sundays, faithfully, unfailingly, across all the parishes of
christendom, the pastors have done this [for] the holy common
people of God.[2]

Whatever I may feel about some of the theology implied in
this passage, I still find it intensely moving to read, and it
restores in me a sense of proportion when I'm tempted to
think that the twentieth century in England is all that has
ever really existed. To discover a continuity with the past
can save us from all kinds of arrogance, and the use of
liturgy can be one of the most powerful ways of doing so.

2. Liturgy and belonging

Not only does liturgy provide us with continuity
'vertically' through history; it also helps us to be aware of
belonging 'horizontally' to the body of Christ throughout
the world. There has been much debate recently in
Anglican churches about the issue of 'Common Prayer'. It

used to be the case (in mythology, if not in reality) that you could go into any Anglican church anywhere in Britain (or indeed the world) and experience the *Book of Common Prayer* liturgy using exactly the same words, readings and actions. This was thought to hold together Anglicans as a family, and even if it was only ever a bit of a myth, there still was a strongly recognisable family likeness.

But now that liturgical revision has given us a plethora of alternatives and options, there has been a great degree of concern in some circles about the loss of this common prayer. Liturgists are working hard at defining what does make an act of worship 'Anglican', and the emerging emphasis is on doing this in ways that are not *text*-based but *shape*-based. Even if all the words we use in liturgical services are not necessarily verbatim with other branches of the Church, the shape of our worship is pretty similar, and is recognisably the same in many different countries and denominations. I can go to an Anglican service elsewhere in England or the world and find myself at home and familiar with what is going on. And when I use liturgy on home territory, I am reminded of my brothers and sisters worshipping in mud huts or cathedrals around the world. Here again our culture is ambivalent: the so-called 'global village' created by the communications revolution means that we can be very aware of what is going on round the world, and yet modern-day fragmentation means that we often only ever think of ourselves, and regard what we do and the way we do it as the 'real thing'. Liturgical worship reminds us forcefully that we are just one small tribe in a worldwide family of those who have set their hearts on following the Lord who came for every nation, tribe and tongue. That has to be good for us!

3. Liturgy and time

Another function of living in a post-modern world is the

pressure of time. In past societies (or at least in our idealised pictures of them) there was a rhythm of work, leisure and rest which were fairly (if rather unequally) distinguished from one another. But now with the rise of technology which means that we are perpetually available to one another, and the increased competitiveness in the commercial world which means longer working hours simply in order to survive, professional people and others fortunate enough to have any work at all are feeling the pinch of time coming at them from everywhere all at the same time. Work, family, church and expectations from everyone, all compete to squeeze us in a vice-like grip. The result of this is that when we do relax we try to do so in 'decompressed time'; in other words we try to do what we can to step outside the pressure of time's flow.

Worship, too, can feel like a pressure, and so there has been a rise of styles which seek to relieve some of the tension and make the whole thing feel more relaxed. Jeremy Begbie has shown how the increasingly popular music of John Tavener seeks to create this decompressed time through musical structures which subvert teleology.[3] In other words there is nothing which speaks of a progress through time from a beginning towards an ending, but just a timeless oasis for us to relax in. The gentle style of music influenced by Celtic spirituality has a similar effect, as does the hypnotic repetition of Taizé chants, and styles such as these can indeed provide relaxation and rest in a hectic world.

But there is a danger. If our worship takes place too much in decompressed time, we can easily begin to believe that decompressed time is where God meets us, rather than in the hustle and bustle of whatever each day holds for us. At the extreme, this theology of life can lead us to withdrawal from the world rather than engagement with it, a criticism frequently levelled (rightly or wrongly) at over-pietistic charismatics. That is why God has chosen to reveal himself to us in the context of real time, and through the medium of story. The history of God's creation, saving acts and eventual winding up of time into eternity provide a story of which we are a part, and our lives, however busy they may be, are chapters from the story. Yes, we do at times need to share with our Father the silence of eternity, but we also need to meet him amid the panic of modern life. It is right that for periods of our worship time stands still for us, but we also need something to drive us forward. The temptation to build tents and stay where we are has always been a strong one, and yet Jesus' voice is heard again pushing us forward to meet God in the next event.

Jesus' voice can be heard most strongly, I believe, through a liturgical framework for our worship. The shape of the service, provided by the liturgy, moves us from a starting point, via a middle, towards an end. We may pause on the journey, but we are never allowed to abandon it altogether. Thus worship provides not an escape but rather a re-engagement with the 'real world out there'.

4. Liturgy and Scripture

It has often been said, perhaps with some degree of justification, that charismatics are highly selective in their use of biblical themes for their spirituality. There can be an emphasis, it is claimed, on triumph and victory, with little on defeat, failure or suffering; or the Spirit receives front-page headlines while the Father is relegated to the small print somewhere. Personally I think there is more caricature here than truth (although even if I am triumphalistic I'd rather be so than have the liberal 'death-wish' so much in evidence elsewhere), but there probably isn't smoke with a total absence of fire. That is why we need the liturgical resources of *calendar* and *lectionary*.

A lectionary, built in to the worship of most liturgical churches, is a series of Bible readings set for each day of the year. The idea is that by the use of the lectionary both in public worship at services and in the daily devotions of individuals, a maximum range of biblical passages is covered, including the difficult bits which we might otherwise avoid. The calendar marks the different liturgical seasons and times, such as Lent, Advent, Pentecost, and so on, when different events in God's action in the world are celebrated, as well as providing opportunities to celebrate and learn from the lives of his saints down the ages. Different times in the calendar would obviously pick up appropriate passages and themes from Scripture in the lectionary.

If charismatics, who place a high value on the immediacy of the Spirit and the latest thing he is saying to the churches, can easily become over-selective when it comes to the Bible, the use of the lectionary and calendar can help us avoid this dangerous error and become more well-rounded in our use of Scripture. We can avoid concentrating again and again on the same familiar parts of the Bible, and neglecting those which may have much to say but which are less readily accessible.

So if charismatics are traditionally good at doing Easter, how are we at Good Friday? And if we're good at doing Ascension and Pentecost, what do we make of the following week when Trinity Sunday comes along, with the theological depth required there? What about the seasons of the church's year: can we live with the need to be less than exuberant for the duration of Lent, so that the celebration of Easter will be so much more meaningful? I remember a service on the third Sunday in Advent (just in the run up to Christmas) when we were led in worship by someone who had chosen a song of celebration for 'the resurrection of the Lord'. Yes, Jesus is risen, even in Advent, but that wasn't what we were about then. We wouldn't sing 'Thine be the glory' on Good Friday (would we?): it's pre-empting the end of the story, even though we know what that ending is and that it is inexorably coming.

Before I gave it up one Lent, I used to be an avid watcher of a certain soap opera set not far from the city of London. It was filmed on a set which was in the parish of a friend of mine, and each episode was made approximately six weeks before it was broadcast. This presented great problems with some of the backgrounds: the vegetation in the Square would have been perpetually behind the rest of the country. So apparently they employed a team of 'gardeners' who had to tie leaves onto the trees in early spring, six weeks before the proper ones were going to appear, so that things were not out of synch with the real world.

Renewal has this tendency to make things happen before they're ready. Why can't we let it be winter while it needs to be? Why can't we live with the austerity of Lent before we get too happy about Easter, or with the penitence of Advent before the joy of Christmas? The spirit of our age is to want instant gratification: the old slogan for Access cards, 'Taking the waiting out of wanting', was in many ways the motto for a generation, and charismatics have been infected heavily by it.

So the use of the Bible in liturgical worship can provide a helpful corrective to tendencies such as these. However, quite apart from the readings set within the liturgy, the texts themselves contain much that is either directly or implicitly biblical. By repeating bits of liturgy we are in fact using biblical material, so we are fed on Scripture both ways. There is no dichotomy between being liturgical and being biblical: the two really do go together hand in hand.

5. Liturgy and doctrine

Tied in with this is the way in which liturgy can help us to become doctrinally well-balanced. Different churches handle their doctrine in different ways. Some work with 'Confessions' or 'Statements of Faith' – short statements which try to encapsulate or sum up the particular beliefs of the denomination in question. While the Anglican catechism tried to do this in the past for those new to the faith, it is generally accepted that in the Church of England our doctrine is enshrined in our liturgy. The 1974 Worship and Doctrine Measure, which sets out this principle, states that 'The doctrine of the Church of England... is to be found in the Thirty Nine Articles of Religion, the *Book of Common Prayer*, and the Ordinal'.

So when a member of the clergy is being instituted to a new parish or job, their oath that 'in public prayer and administration of the sacraments I will use only the forms of service which are authorised or allowed by canon', is not so much a liturgical promise as a doctrinal one. As we saw in the last chapter, this use of liturgy for doctrine is one which goes right back to the practice of the early church.

Now I am not in any sense wanting to suggest that being Anglican is a cast-iron guarantee of doctrinal soundness, but I do believe that it is harder to go off the wall if liturgy is a part of your worship, particularly if that liturgy is not just homegrown but is the product of denominational specialists. Just as Wesley recognised the fact that people learned their theology not from what they heard preached in sermons but from what they sang in hymns, so Anglicans very often are shaped spiritually by the liturgy they use week by week.

6. Liturgy and clarity

Liturgy can help us to articulate clearly what it is we are trying to say. One of the worst services I've ever been to was a service of infant dedication in a Free church. I do find it interesting that the Free Churches turn to liturgy for the important occasions, but the way it was used in this particular instance was, to my mind, amateurish in the extreme. Most of it, although liturgical in feel and style, seemed to be being made up as it went along, apart from

one or two vague promises which the parents were asked to
make about something or other. As the service progressed I
amused myself by imagining that I was an alien who had
just dropped in, and was trying to work out exactly the
theology of dedication the service was selling, the biblical
precedent they felt they had for it, and what difference the
ceremony was supposed to have made to whom. I failed. As
far as I could see the service was simply a set of mutually
contradictory messages, half-formed theological ideas, and
Bible verses which had something to do with children. I'm
not saying, of course, that convinced Free Church people
have no coherent theology of dedication, just that this
service did nothing to tell me what it was.

I couldn't help but contrast the Anglican equivalent.
Quite apart from the differences in theology, the liturgy
explains exactly what is going on, why we think it's biblical,
and what exactly we think we're doing. The use of set texts
for occasions like this leaves no one in any doubt about
matters like these. Even if Free Church people reject the
theology, at least they know what it is they are rejecting!
Liturgy does seem to be important at the times of so-called
'rites of passage' (births, marriages and deaths), as
evidenced by the fact that churches which would be very
antagonistic towards it the rest of the time suddenly get out
a prayer book, dust it off and use it. Carefully written
words, repeated on each occasion, do seem to have a special
place at times like these. Even secular 'services' (such as
registry office weddings) use liturgy, presumably because
we need words to say what we mean. So why not enhance
all of our worship with such words, enshrined in the
church's liturgy?

7. Liturgy and economy

Our church administrator has a daughter who, when she
married, left the Church of England and moved into a

seriously non-liturgical church. Every now and then she comes home to stay with Mum and attends one of our services. On one occasion she explained how much she enjoyed these returns to her Anglican roots, not least because 'not once in the whole of the Anglican liturgy does it say "just really"'. Little bits of jargon such as this which are common in earnest church circles have an important function: they allow the person praying off the top of their head a little thinking time while they mentally compose the next sentence. Useful though this may be, it can become a bit tiresome to those listening (once in a time of extreme boredom I counted the word 'Lord' forty-six times in a single prayer). I am all for extempore prayer, but liturgy has a value because in praying with the carefully thought out and set down words of others we are set free from repetitive jargon and interminable rambling around the point. If I want a chat with a friend I'll ring them up and we'll just natter, but if I want, for example, to apply for a job or complain about something to a company, I'll write a letter, so that I can think through what it is I want to say and set it down with clarity and economy. It's great to natter to God at times, but in public worship it is appropriate as it were to write him liturgical letters, so that everyone can see quickly what we're getting at and agree by saying 'Amen' at the end. I've often joined dutifully in the 'Amen' at the end of extempore prayers without being at all clear what it is I'm agreeing with. The use of liturgy can bring this kind of economy to our worship, making it more accessible to the uninitiated and less boring to the regulars. Jargon-free services really are possible, apart of course from the jargon contained in the liturgy, but at least each bit is only there once!

8. Liturgy and poetry

Never in my wildest dreams would I describe myself as an

artist (neither, I notice, would anyone else!), although I did once paint the downstairs loo. But from my limited experience as a composer of music and an erstwhile writer of angst-ridden adolescent poetry, I am convinced of one important principle: the spontaneous is rarely the best. I'm sure those who do have artistic streaks (like those on the paintwork in my loo) would agree that there is very little which cannot be improved by reworking, editing or even scrapping altogether. The art of writing liturgy is no different. Let me say again that I am all for the spontaneous in worship, and I believe that those who can only ever talk to God in ancient words may be severely handicapped in their relationship with him, but I am concerned for churches which only ever do things spontaneously, because they are probably using less than the best. Although I haven't been directly involved, I do know something of the process by which Anglican liturgical texts are produced and refined. I know that it can be highly time-consuming and frustrating, but when the finished product finally does appear, I can be confident that it is the best it can be. Never to worship with words which have been through this polishing process is to use the perpetually sub-standard.

9. Liturgy and order

This may just be a strange quirk of mine, and you certainly wouldn't believe it if you saw either my desk or my garden, but I do actually prefer order to chaos. The same is true of worship, and the use of liturgy can bring a pleasing order to an otherwise seemingly random series of events.

Let me give you a couple of examples. We've already mentioned the shape of the Anglican services which provides a logical sense of flow and progress through time. In the Communion service, for example, we come into God's presence, acknowledging the help we need even to do that, we get right with him after all the wrong things which have been a part of our lives over the past week, we listen to his word read and explained, we bring to him our needs in intercession, and we approach his table to receive the bread and wine which will strengthen us to go out and live for him during the coming week. This isn't the only way of doing things, but it is a good way, and it does make sense. There is a sense of logical flow which, when removed, can make services which are supposedly 'open to the Spirit' seem just a bit arbitrary in the way they happen. Sometimes you can almost hear the worship leader thinking 'What shall we do next?' To put our worship in this kind of framework so that we journey through it, and so that past, present and future are integrated in a logical way, can be very helpful.

My second example is from one part within a Communion service, and will require a little explanation for those unfamiliar with the principles. There is in the service a 'Eucharistic prayer' or prayer of thanksgiving over the bread and wine, which contains a paragraph called the 'proper preface'. This preface is an optional section in which appropriate words may be inserted during different seasons and for different occasions and festivals. Because its doctrine is, as we have seen, enshrined in the liturgy, the Church of England jealously guards the form of these prayers and their 'proper' insertions. It is illegal to use in Anglican worship any Eucharistic prayer which is unauthorised. However, my liturgical work allows me to do a little bit of occasional road-testing of up-and-coming liturgical texts. A prayer which was proposed at one stage sought to encourage the feel that the whole church (and not just the vicar) is praying by allowing the proper preface to consist of spontaneous interjections from the congregation (who said liturgy was set, staid and formal?). I decided it would be good to try this one out.

The Lord in his great wisdom and mercy has given two precious gifts to the church: Lent and August. These are special periods when you can get away with just about anything without anyone complaining; in Lent because we're all meant to be miserable anyway, and in August because we're all absent on holiday and the church is full of visitors who don't know any better. So we use these periods to experiment, and one August I gave a wandering radio mike to one of the servers and encouraged anyone who wanted to do so to stick up a hand and speak out a one-sentence prayer of thanksgiving to God for some aspect of his character, some blessing from the previous week, or whatever, in the 'proper preface' slot. But I asked them all to begin their prayers with the phrase 'And now we give you thanks...', words with which they were familiar since they formed the usual introduction to the prefaces. I put up an OHP slide with 'And now we give you thanks...' on it, people duly performed, and it went well and felt good, but the repeated use of that introductory formula made the whole thing sound much more like a piece of liturgical worship and less as if we'd stopped the service and started a prayer meeting instead. This kind of order felt pleasing, and the mixture of liturgy and spontaneity which emerged was just the kind of thing for which I will be arguing throughout this book.

10. Liturgy and children

I have written elsewhere about worship with children,[4] and long experience with our children and others' has shown that liturgy is a highly effective means of drawing them into God's presence. In our family, Steve, when he was only five, and not yet very good at reading words like 'troll' and 'porridge', could handle the Rite A confession with no trouble, 'negligence', 'weakness' and 'deliberate fault' included. And his little brother Paul, who was three, not only learned the entire *Gloria* off by heart, but could also sing it to the setting we used on Sundays. They had their own children's Communion book, of which they were very proud, and Paul, even though he could as yet only recognise words like 'look', 'and', 'the' and 'doggy' (the latter of which features only minimally in the text of Rite A), he 'read' it intently as he sang his little heart out, sometimes even managing to have the book the right way up. They may not have understood every last theological nuance of the words, but then neither did their mum and dad. We were all learning together, and we continue to do so to this day.

Why do children find liturgy so helpful and attractive? Because they are supremely liturgical creatures. Our two-year-old daughter is a prime example. Each bedtime there is a liturgy we have to go through, which consists, like all liturgies, of both words and action. First she has to say goodnight to Samuel (her little friend from Sheffield) and give his photo a kiss. Then we go outside into the hall, pausing to say goodnight to the cross and the picture of Bart Simpson which adorn my study door. Then upstairs to the landing window for a 'goodnight' to the Archdeacon who lives opposite. Thence to her bedroom, where we have to say goodnight to the funny man on her 'Don't worry, be happy' poster. Then to the jingly sheep mobile, the elephant-shaped lampshade, and the clowns hanging above her cot, one of which, of her choosing, is fortunate enough to get a kiss. Finally she'll nestle into my shoulder while we talk to Jesus, and then we wind up Musicman, who plays a tinkly tune while she goes to sleep. None of that has actually been authorised by General Synod (except possibly the Archdeacon), but if it isn't liturgy I don't know what is! As Vicki grows up, her life will continue to be liturgical. At school she will do skipping rhymes in the playground. She may well join the Brownies and Guides, two other highly liturgical organisations. Children function consistently with all kinds of liturgy in their lives, so why on earth should we expect their worship in church to be any different? Yet so often we have robbed them of this rich resource because we patronisingly feel it is 'beyond them'.

We had a very formative experience in this area when our boys were about six and four. A friend was being ordained in Sheffield Cathedral and the family was invited. We groaned on receiving the invitation: what on earth were we going to do with the kids through that lot? Everyone was going, so we couldn't leave them with a babysitter. They'd just have to come with us and we'd take them out when they got fed up during the first hymn and we'd play in the churchyard. But much to our surprise they were fascinated by the service, and in particular two elements within it: the movement and processions of all the ministers and choir in their colourful robes, and the sung litany. A litany is a way of praying which uses spoken or sung paragraphs with a short repeated response from the congregation. By about the fourth response the boys were joining in lustily with the rest of the congregation. So many of the things which we find emotionally unfriendly and formal can be the very things which our youngsters love and which can draw them into involvement. It's a tragedy when we edit them out of our church life. We need to work hard at child-friendly liturgy, and avoid what I believe has been a large mistake sometimes made by the all-age worship lobby, the scrapping of it altogether.

11. Liturgy and liberty

As you will see more and more as you progress through this book I am all for an openness to the spontaneous and the moving of the Spirit during a service of worship, but I am convinced that to be open is not necessarily to be chaotic. We've already seen a restorationist understanding of the place of liturgy in the quotation about 2 Chronicles 5: in some churches you do get the impression that a service is *really* spiritual when everything you've planned goes out of the window. Personally I would find it a highly frustrating way to work, and I suspect that rather than being highly spiritual this approach just shows a lack of listening to God during the planning process!

Obviously liturgy *can* be fixed, formal and restrictive to the life of the Spirit. This book comes out of a burning conviction that it needn't be. The view of liturgy which we so often unconsciously adopt is that it is a cage which shuts us in, keeps us locked up, and stops us from going anywhere. But I believe we can learn to see liturgy not as a cage but as scaffolding which can help support what we're building, and give it strength, shape and stability. Another picture would be the image in Ezekiel 37, which has nothing whatsoever to do with liturgy but is still highly evocative. If the parched bones littering the desert speak of the spiritual dryness and deadness of the nation, I find it interesting that the Lord doesn't tell the son of man to leave them where they are and prophesy into being a nation of jellyfish instead. Rather he begins with the bones, forming them into skeletons, and then clothing them with flesh and finally life. Much liturgical worship may still be at a rather rattly stage, but my conviction is that flesh and spirit need something to hang on to. This book is an attempt to rescue the bones and reclothe them with the life of the Spirit, and this chapter is meant to convince you that to do so is a worthwhile exercise.

12. Liturgy and inevitability

My final point is that whether we like it or not our worship will tend to become liturgical. However much we may say we hate liturgy, we will have it. The Baptist church in which I was brought up probably typifies this; we were definitely *not* liturgical, but every week without fail the service went like this: Hymn – Prayer – Reading – Hymn – Notices – Collection – Very Long Prayer – Hymn – Sermon – Hymn

– Benediction (of the non-conformist, not the Anglo-Catholic variety, of course). The same phenomenon is to be found in other events not know for their Anglican feel; a Vineyard service, a Billy Graham crusade or a Pentecostal revival meeting all have their set structure and often their verbal traditions too.

I am not so arrogant as to believe that the Church of England is God's way of doing things, but I do firmly believe that liturgy is God's way of doing things. Otherwise why would he have built into us such a tendency towards it? I was taught liturgy at college by the late Geoffrey Cuming, a famous Anglican scholar, and I'll always remember his very first lecture, in which he talked about 'personal liturgies' – the way we always tie one shoelace up before the other (not that many of us can tie both up at once: I think he meant that we invariably start with the same one, left or right) or begin shaving in the morning with the same side of the face each day (this was before the days of women's ordination in the Church of England). He talked as well about secular community liturgies, like the kind of chants which occur at football matches (so I've been told), or the singing of 'Auld Lang Syne' on New Year's Eve, or 'Happy Birthday to You'.

Even a trip to McDonald's is a highly liturgical event: you fight your way through the crowd where you are confronted by a pimply teenager who bellows in your face 'HELLO I'M TRACEY HOW CAN I HELP YOU?' (Be honest – haven't you always wanted to shout back? 'HELLO TRACEY I'D LIKE A BIG MAC AND REGULAR FRIES PLEASE'? And another thing: why are they always called Tracey?) You see, it's a liturgical world out there, and we're all wired up as liturgical creatures who run on repetition and habit. And when you think about it, how could there be anything new if there was nothing old, or anything spontaneous if there was nothing planned? So why on earth should we believe we can dispense with liturgy, even if we wanted to, in the context of worship? Instead of doing so while fooling ourselves into believing we're not, why shouldn't we use liturgy deliberately and proudly, with the best, most carefully prepared resources available, and with all the creativity we can muster? How can we do that, while still giving the Holy Spirit the freedom to move among us in sovereign power? That's what this book is all about. It was written out of a conviction that liturgy and liberty can not only work together, but also belong together, and it was written from the context of a church where its principles were being worked out in practice, as they have been in other churches too. It is offered to the body of Christ in the hope that it will help us to worship in spirit and in truth; so here goes. We must begin by asking the question 'Who is equal to this task?' What does a leader of renewed liturgical worship look like?

Notes

1 A simplified version of the diagram in Andrew Walker, *Restoring the Kingdom* (London: Hodder & Stoughton, 1985) p 133. Walker quotes this in turn from *Restoration* magazine, Nov/Dec 1983, p 40.

2 Gregory Dix, *The Shape of the Liturgy* (Westminster: Dacre, 1945) p 744.

3 J. Begbie, 'Theology through Music: Tavener, Time and Eternity' in D. F. Ford and D. L. Stamps (eds), *Essentials of Christian Community* (Edinburgh: T & T Clark, 1996) pp 23-26.

4 John and Chris Leach, *And for Your Children* (Crowborough: Monarch, 1994).

4

The Worship Leader –

A Job Description

If the previous chapters accurately describe something of what we expect to happen when we worship, and some of the ways in which we may expect it to happen, it is clear that the role of the leader in worship is a very important one indeed. A tremendous amount hangs on his or her ability to handle things well, and at the very least not to get in the way of what God is trying to do. In this chapter we'll spend some time looking at the role of the worship leader, first at just what that role involves, and then at what sort of person he or she must be to lead God's people successfully in worship. I want to suggest, in fact, that a worship leader, whether an ordained minister or a lay leader, has not one role but nine. Throughout this section I'll use the pronoun 'he', on the understanding that this is for the sake of brevity rather than discrimination. Clearly the job spec does not involve being male!

1. Figurehead

Those who have been on management training courses and gone through the exercise of being left in a group without a leader will know just what an uncomfortable situation that is. Valuable though it may be in some settings, it is certainly not what we want worshippers to experience. If I had to identify one thing which makes for successful worship, it would be *security* for the congregation, both in God himself and also in the leader. Therefore the leader needs to inspire that sort of confidence in people, and needs to be in a position, both physically and spiritually, to be seen to be able to inspire it. On a purely physical level, he should be in a place where all can see him as he will provide a focus of attention, at least for the beginning of the worship time, and he must never desert his post while the worship continues, since if anything untoward happens, all eyes will instantly be on him to get direction about how to cope. If you open your eyes and return from a state of rapture because of an interruption to find that the leader is somewhere in the fifteenth row, it doesn't help your security one little bit. On a spiritual level, if the leader is not the vicar or minister he must be known to be a person of maturity who is held in esteem by the church leadership.

2. Host

Whether you are talking about a regular Sunday church service, a Saturday night ecumenical Celebration, or a small fellowship group in someone's front room, somebody needs to be seen to be hosting the occasion. This may involve such things as welcoming people, making sure they are comfortable, having all the right books, knowing where the loos are, and so on. This won't always fall to the lot of the lay worship leader, but it may well do occasionally, especially in a gathering where he is to open the proceedings. If he is the first person to be seen or heard on the platform, the congregation will look to him for some kind of practical help to feel a part of what is going on. Like any good host, he needs to be polite and attentive to people's comfort while at the same time resisting the temptation to become the life and soul of the party.

3. Articulator

By this rather ugly term I simply mean one who says for people what they are thinking or feeling in order to establish some kind of bond between himself and them and between different members of the congregation. This may range from 'Isn't it good to come together to praise the Lord?' at one end of the spectrum to something like 'Many of us may be finding it difficult to think of praising God after those tragic riots in our city last night. This kind of thing raises all sorts of questions for us, but we're here today because we know that only God can make any sense at all of the evil in our world. So let's offer him a sacrifice of praise.' It really involves catching the mood of the gathering, being aware of what may be going on for people, and making sure that we worship through these feelings, not simply laying them aside if they don't seem to fit.

This principle came home to me strongly one Sunday morning when I had to lead worship in our parish church. It was just like any other Sunday morning, except for the fact that the day before nearly a hundred people had been killed in the disaster at Hillsborough football ground, about three miles away. Some of the congregation had been up all night trying to keep crushed bodies alive or comforting bereaved relatives. And there was I, trying to invite people to come with praise and thanksgiving to a God of love and mercy. I don't know how well I did, but I do know that only the grace of God helped me on that occasion. A good vicar or minister should naturally have this pastoral feel for the congregation, but a lay leader, or any leader who is working in a context other than his own church, may find it more difficult. This task, if done sensitively, can free charismatic worship from its alleged bugbear of triumphalism, but if it is ignored it can leave people behind or alienate them totally.

4. Encourager

After articulating for people the place they are at, the next task is to move them on into worship. Many people will come feeling that worshipping is only a marginally more attractive prospect at the moment than setting fire to their trousers. Many will come full of inhibitions and self-consciousness. Some will be there for the first time and will feel very uncertain of the whole thing. All will need to be encouraged to enter fully into the experience of worship, not just once at the beginning, but often, as new depths of intimacy with God are reached. Whether the need is for encouragement to relax physically, to sing in the Spirit or to contribute prophetically, the leader is the person to do it, with gentleness and tact.

5. Leader

This aspect of the role almost goes without mention, but not quite. The point needs to be made that a leader is someone who goes out first into the fray in order that others may follow. Yet one occasionally meets clergy and worship leaders who, like the famous Duke of Plaza-Toro, find it less exciting to lead from behind. Clergy particularly may have a tendency to 'preside' over the gathering in a way which suggests that they are not really involved at grass-roots level. It's important to lead people, not push them or manipulate them, in all sorts of areas of leadership; in worship it's absolutely essential. It's no good encouraging people by saying, in effect, 'Come on, for goodness sake, someone get a prophecy!' You'll always need to lead by example. People don't relax and enter into worship simply by being told to; what will help more than anything is for them to see the leader relaxed and enjoying himself. As a general rule, you won't get people to go anywhere you're not prepared to go to yourself.

6. Protector

People approach worship, perhaps especially charismatic worship, with all sorts of anxieties and fears. These are mostly unnamed and unfaced, but if really pressed people might admit to worrying, in their weaker moments, about things like false manifestations of gifts, demons appearing (perhaps even in them!), other interruptions in the service from disturbed people or, more vaguely, about things getting 'out of control' in some unspecified way. The congregation need to feel protected from anything which they see as being potentially harmful to them, and the leader needs to give them this security. Again lay leaders may have to work harder here than clergy, since they may not immediately command the same respect. Also, since people's fears are not all of negative things, there is the need for the leader to take on the role of what I call the 'priest'.

7. Priest

It can truly be a fearful thing to fall into the hands of the living God, and since our expectations about what might happen in worship have been raised to include such physical manifestations as laughing, screaming, weeping or resting in the Spirit (or 'falling over' as we theologians call it), it can seem as frightening at times when God gets his hands on you as when the Enemy does. Thus the leader, in the twin role of protector and priest, must understand the ways both of God and the Enemy (as well, of course, as the disturbed or even just overenthusiastic human spirit), discern which is which, and help the people accordingly to resist or go with whatever is happening. As the congregation will immediately look to the leader to see how to react if anything untoward or unplanned occurs, he must above all be someone who does not panic, since there are few things more infectious in a group. He will need to be able to deal quickly and decisively with an unhelpful contribution in worship, while at the same time dealing gently and lovingly with the person who brought it. He will need to be able to show that he understands what God is doing in dramatic events, and that he is happy to be a part of that. He will also need to have the help of a ministry team experienced, as he is, in dealing with people under the unction of the Holy Spirit or in the grip of the demonic, since he must not leave his position up front to deal with crises in the congregation. His other roles don't stop just because someone screams, and it will make people feel very insecure indeed if there is no figurehead.

There is also a task for the leader as 'priest' to do in the area of discernment. They say it's an ill wind which blows nobody any good, and the particular breeze which has been blowing in from Toronto for the last few years has certainly benefited authors (including myself!) from all sides. Recently there has been a crop of books explaining why this whole business is not a move of God but rather a satanic delusion or at best an exercise in human 'hysteria' or 'hypnotism'. While there is no doubt much that is sensationalist and inaccurate in such writings (including the use of the term 'hysteria' in this context) there are things which devotees of the 'Blessing' need to hear and take note of. Of particular concern to its opponents is the tacit assumption that whatever happens is God at work and is therefore to be encouraged. While God can indeed move in some pretty mysterious ways, the fact is that people can too, and so the leader up front will need to discern which behaviour needs to be encouraged, which may be tolerated, and which needs stopping. This kind of discernment makes the task harder than simply blessing everything which is going on, but I believe it is a task which needs doing. The leader as 'priest' is the person to do it.

I feel that I need to emphasise what I don't mean by the word 'priest' in this context. Of course Jesus is our great

High Priest, and we have no need of any other mediator between us and God. Neither am I referring specifically to the ordained clergy; this will of course be part of his priestly role, but I will say more about him under the next heading. What I mean is simply that the worship leader, whether lay or ordained, is one who fits in with the Old Testament picture of priests – those who understood what God did since, to put it simply, they spent time with him for a living. This concept is one which I find helpful. The shaman or witch-doctor fulfils this role in other religions and cultures, and despite the accessibility of our God to all his people, I feel that there is still a role for those who especially understand God in interpreting for less mature believers exactly what is going on. This role will be especially important as God's people gather for worship with the express aim of experiencing his presence and power among them. And we mustn't forget that at times the power of God will be so strong that even the priests are sent scuttling out of the way!

8. President

Tied in very much with the role of the priest is that of the 'president', a term used helpfully in the Anglican liturgy to describe the role of the priest in the celebration of the Eucharist. The background for this is the Jewish celebration of the Passover, where the family patriarch would naturally assume the leading role at the head of the table, presiding over the ceremony and holding the different contributions together. Particular prayers and actions would appropriately be said and done by him alone, and he would provide some sort of focus for the whole group. I find it helpful to think of the priest celebrating the sacraments as having a similar role, coming both from his position *vis-à-vis* God because of his ordination, and his position *vis-à-vis* the congregation because of his pastoral care and leadership. And I would see this role extending to those types of service which, although not classed by the Thirty Nine Articles as 'sacraments', nevertheless have something 'sacramental' about them. The minister officiating for example at weddings or funerals still has the job of 'presiding' over the event in a way which facilitates worship among those present. Even in non-conformist churches where less emphasis may be placed on the sacramental side of worship, there is still the need for someone to preside at the Lord's Table – either the minister himself or a deacon or elder. So the president's role is an important one, whether or not it is seen directly in terms of priesthood and ordination.

9. Prophet

I mean by this term the ability to function 'prophetically' rather than simply to function as a 'prophet'. In other words it's not so much about contributing a prophecy from time to time, although this is an important part of it, but more about the much broader prophetic ability to convey to his people the heart of God. I see it much more in the 'Old Testament' sense of the prophet who was able to read the signs of the times and see them from God's perspective. There need be no tension here, however, between the concepts of 'Old Testament' and 'New Testament' or 'charismatic' prophecy. Although there are some obvious differences, the overwhelming similarity seems to be the ability of the prophet to hear from God about how he sees things and to communicate that sense to the people. Whether he shouts at the king, writes it in a book or offers it at a charismatic prayer meeting seems to me to be secondary. A leader needs to be able to feel what God is doing during a time of worship, where he is taking people, and how confidently they are following him. This may then need to be communicated to the people in such a way that they are put in touch with the mind and purposes of God. If we were working with a very simple model of worship like equating it, for example, with adoration only, there would be little need for this role to be fulfilled. But since in this book at least we are thinking of a very diverse set of pathways down which we may be led by the Spirit during a worship time, we do need someone who, under the anointing of that Spirit, can act to some extent as a guide for the journey.

Many churches find it a helpful process to write job descriptions for each person involved in any ministry within the life of the church, from the vicar to the deputy-washer-of-tea-towels. Not only does this help people to know exactly what they are committing themselves to when they take on a job, but it also gives a clearer picture of the sort of person who might do that job successfully. If the roles we have described above form part of the job description of the worship leader, can we now move on to see what sort of person might be right for the job? If these are the tasks, who might be equal to them? Again, I've identified several different characteristics of the good worship leader, and I have made no attempt to tie them in properly with the roles above. The fact that once again I've managed to think of nine of them is purely coincidental.

1. Maturity

It will be clear from what we've said before that leading worship will not be a new Christian's first task after coming to faith. Clergy and lay leaders alike will need a thorough biblical grounding, a sound knowledge of theology, and a real live experience of God in their own lives. In worship supremely we are dealing with a God who reveals himself in truth, and we will need to be dealing with truths as we worship. Doctrine is important, therefore, not as a dry academic study to keep the cupboards in our brains well stocked, but as a living knowledge of just who God is so that we can encounter him in truth as well as in spirit. The need for this kind of deep understanding is especially reinforced when we realise that it's not just God who is involved in our worship; the Enemy is there too, flitting around the edges, trying to see if he can get a grip in order to pervert us and lead us off into erroneous side-lines. As the leader is involved in encouraging others in worship, he constantly needs to apply the plumb-line of good biblical doctrine to every contribution, including his own, in order to ensure that everything is straight. I'm not saying that you need a PhD in theology before you can be a good worship leader, but you do need the depth of understanding and knowledge which takes years rather than weeks to acquire. A faithful walk with the Lord over a long period, and a steady growth in biblical study and understanding are vital here, and will prevent a congregation being led off into side-lines or even error.

2. Experience

I wanted to be a van driver in my youth, but whenever I applied for a job it was always the same: 'Have you got any driving experience? No? Sorry.' Only when I had broken into the business by devious means which need not concern us now could I hold my head up in van-driving circles as a fully experienced member of the club. These catch-22 situations can be avoided in the church if we take seriously Jesus' method of modelling and discipling. A good rule for a church (although one which is not easy to keep) is that no one from the vicar down does anything without having someone else there who is being trained to do it themselves. This rule certainly ought to apply in the worship group, and even in the leadership of the whole service. It may not be appropriate or even legal for lay people to lead every part, but there are things which they can do, and potential leaders should be given training in doing them.

John Wimber has helpfully spelled out what he sees to be Jesus' method of modelling; although he gleans this primarily from the healing ministry in the Gospels and Acts, it can be applied to just about any area of church life. First Jesus did it, then he did it with trainees watching, then they did it with him watching, and then he left them to do it on their own. Perhaps the most striking example of this in action can be seen by comparing the accounts of Jesus raising Jairus' daughter (Luke 8) with the raising of Dorcas by Peter in Acts 9. Peter is clearly following the model he had seen Jesus use. If we are to take this method of modelling seriously in our church life we must beware of two common errors: first, we mustn't forget the need for feedback and critical assessment of the trainees' performance. Those of us who are British find this difficult and embarrassing, and so we often omit it. If things have gone well we may make an encouraging comment, but if not we prefer to put the whole experience behind us and never ever talk about it again for as long as we live. While understandable, this approach does mean that we rob ourselves of an important opportunity for growth and learning, so we need gently to encourage one another to ask questions like 'Why exactly was it such a horribly disastrous flop?' and 'What might we have done differently?' It is hard to begin with, but gradually to build up a church culture of constructive criticism in an encouraging context will be much more healthy.

Secondly, we must be prepared for the fact that sometimes the trainees we're working with will reach the point where their skill level passes our own, as they begin to do greater works even than we can manage. We need to rejoice in this and encourage them to keep going for it, rather than get defensive and hypercritical. In other words, to be good trainers we need to be non-threatening and non-threatened.

If we are modelling our worship skills the new leader standing up to front a worship slot will not be beginning from scratch, as it were, but will already have served an apprenticeship which will have equipped him to deal positively with anything which may happen in worship. If the Spirit falls on someone and they begin weeping, the leader will know what to do since he has seen other, more experienced leaders handle the same thing before. If a demon manifests itself, he will stay calm, since he knows from past experience of seeing someone else handle it that there is nothing to be afraid of. And, most importantly of all, he will have learned from others not just a troubleshooting manual of what to do in 527 different unexpected worship situations, but the skill of listening to God and discerning from him what's going on and how to respond to it. If you are a worship leader, you need to ask yourself now who it is that you are training up to take over when you move on to higher things, and if you are the leader or minister of a church, you might do well to look for other areas where this method of modelling could usefully be employed.

3. Submission

If the worship leader is not the overall church leader, vicar, minister or whatever, he must be someone who is and is seen to be under the authority of that leader. This may sound obvious, but if you stop to think about it, it is in this sort of area that music in worship has had most of its problems historically. If you were to do a survey among Anglican vicars as to who was public enemy number one in their church, how many would say either the organist or the choirmaster? I suspect a very high proportion. I'm not sure whether the same is true in non-conformist circles, but in the Church of England there is often a fierce rivalry between the musical side of the church and its vicar; a rivalry which has been responsible for more than a few nervous breakdowns on both sides. What's the problem? Leaving aside the personalities involved, and trying not to paint every situation too black and white, it seems to me that in a large number of cases what has happened is that music has ceased to be a servant and has become the master. The idea, surely, is that music is used within the service to heighten the liturgy, to raise people's spirits to God, and to provide a vehicle through which people may come in worship before the Lord. But simply because the musical staff are musical, they want things done properly; and because the vicar is perhaps not musical, he abdicates responsibility and lets them get on and do what they want. In the quest for higher musical standards the congregation is left behind as both music and words become more and more complex and Latinate respectively, until you have an esoteric club of musicians and a church which gets the idea of worship that it is simply sitting back and letting it all wash over you (a valid way of worship sometimes, of course, but one which, if indulged in too often, tends to generate the same passive attitude in other areas of church life, such that the whole of Christian discipleship is a matter of letting things wash over you). Music now becomes the ruling force in the church's life (I even know one church where the clergy had to ask the choirmaster whether or not he wanted them to preach a sermon during the service – you can guess what the answer usually was!), and the servant role which music ought to have is totally reversed.

It would be tragic if, within renewed worship, the worship group took on these negative traits previously belonging to the church choir, yet in some places I have seen this beginning to happen in small ways. We must resist it at all costs, and we can do that if worship leaders are in a relationship of submission and love to the church leader,

and always see their work in the context of that servant
role, even if this means at times laying aside some of their
artistic integrity. We do, of course, want a good standard of
music, and I'm not saying we should encourage anything in
our worship to be second rate, but 'good' in the context of
worship doesn't mean 'complicated'; it means first and
foremost 'accessible'. And just as the music needs to be a
servant, so does the music leader. In a previous church I was
in, a visiting preacher said to the congregation (as only a
visiting preacher could have done), 'If you're not
committed to the leader and his wife, and if you don't love
and respect them, then you should leave the church and
find one with leaders whom you can respect.' While this
principle might be a recipe for an ecclesiastical 'all change',
there is certainly truth in it, and I can think of many hassles
which could have been avoided if the advice had been
heeded. Certainly if the music is not going in the same
direction as the rest of the church, trouble is on the
horizon.

I realise that by now many lay worship leaders, or
aspiring ones, will feel like throwing in the towel since they
are in situations where the musical *status quo* is so
entrenched and supported by the church leadership that
their attempt to help the advent of renewal is one long
battle. How can we be in relationships of submission and
love with leaders who don't seem to want to know about
anything which we find so dear to us? This area is a
minefield which I would do well not to step into, but I
would want to say that it is possible, although very difficult
at times, to love and honour those wanting to go in
directions different from our own, and that being in
submission doesn't mean that no creative shaping of one
another's views and ideas is possible. I actually believe that
there is much more potential for changing recalcitrant
leaders within that relationship than there is in a constant
pitched battle.

Since the lay worship leader's job is such a public one, the relationship between him and the church leader will often be on display. He will need not just to be submitted, but to be seen to be. If, for example, the minister needs to step in during a time of worship and take over, the worship leader must be seen to be quite happy for this to happen, rather than scowling or grumbling about it. If you do think it was a mistake, talk about it after the service, don't moan about it at the time. This public face of your relationship is one of the most important aspects of submission.

4. Dedication

The worship leader's tasks require that he is someone who is committed to the job, to those working with him, and to the moving on of the whole church in worship. The church needs to know that he will be there, that he will be there in good time, that he will come prepared, both personally and practically, and that he will put everything he's got into the task in hand, even if he feels that he'd rather be at home watching *Songs of Praise*. Clergy, of course, have little option here, since they are paid to be there, although it is possible to lead worship looking as if you would rather be at home watching *Songs of Praise*. If someone can't be there, the church needs to be sure that he has arranged for the job to be covered adequately. All this, of course, is true for just about any job in the life of the church, but for some worship leaders, especially those with a bit of an artistic temperament, this day-to-day dedication can sometimes be a problem. You may need to redefine your sensitive and creative personality as awkward and sinful at times, and commit yourself to the task anyway.

5. Presence

I find this a very difficult concept to define, although we all know it the instant we see it. It's about the sort of commanding aura that someone either does or doesn't have around them as they stand up in front of a room full of people. Many different things contribute to it: physical size and shape, tone and volume of voice, body language, clothing, confidence and so on. Unfortunately, we have no control whatsoever over some of these. Someone who is six feet four inches tall, with a rich booming voice and a shock of red hair, will naturally tend to have more presence than a five feet two inch balding midget with a squeaky voice, a lisp and a Wolverhampton accent. However the good news, especially for those in the latter category, is that there are some things which you can do to help.

But do we want to? If we must do things to ourselves to make ourselves more conspicuous, isn't that a denial of the whole role of a worship leader? What about 'I must decrease, and he must increase'? There's a real tension here, because while the latter is obviously true, we nevertheless want the congregation to feel as secure as possible during worship, and the more the leader inspires confidence in them the more secure they'll feel. It's not so much a matter of making yourself conspicuous as of coming over confidently and authoritatively. If you naturally have difficulty in doing that, then it seems right to do anything you can which will help. It is possible, as any actor will tell you, to learn not to show nerves, to learn to project your voice, to use your body more effectively and so on. You might try wearing clothes you feel most comfortable in (within the bounds of what is appropriate, obviously!), and you might like to get some friends to give you an honest opinion of how you come over publicly so that you will know which areas need special care. Clergy may need help here too. There is a popular move at least in some church circles away from any clerical 'uniform', including even dog-collars, but there is the need to weigh up the gains in informality against the losses of presence. When all is said and done, a nice gold cope or chasuble can certainly help people to notice that you're there.

I suppose the most helpful definition of presence was one given by a friend, who described it as the ability to stand up in public without making the audience feel nervous for you. I know that our help is in the name of the Lord, but that of itself won't make us immune to normal human nerves. Since anxiety is both so contagious and so counter-productive in worship, we have a duty to do all we can to prevent it from showing.

6. Attractiveness

It is just worth mentioning that presence in itself isn't necessarily a positive characteristic. Count Dracula and Hitler were both oozing with it, but almost certainly wouldn't be the sort of people who could helpfully lead worship in your church. (What do you mean 'Even they'd be an improvement on the current team'?) So our presence must be a positive, attractive thing. There's one key to this, and it never fails: smile a lot. A genuine, open smile can transform any face into a picture which is lovely to look at. If you've had a bad day and can't think of anything to smile about, just concentrate on the goodness and grace of God. You might find that will help your worship in other ways too!

7. Musicality

Well, up to a point. I'll say a bit more about this later, but if the sort of worship you'll be leading involves any music at all, you need at the very least to have some sort of musical feel by which you know whether or not something seems to be right, even if you don't understand why. Certainly if you are going to be leading singing it will be most helpful to the congregation if you are not tone deaf, and if you have the sort of voice which is not that much like a walrus with sinusitis. You certainly don't need to be another Pavarotti, but you do need to be able to stay in tune. If you use an instrument you obviously need to be sufficiently skilled on it so that your playing doesn't get in the way of people's worship.

8. Worship

It seems to me to be axiomatic that you won't lead people any further than you've been yourself. In a very real sense it's true to say that a church's worship will only be as good as that of the worship leader, and that what the worship leader does on the platform or in the pulpit on Sunday will only be as good as what he does during the rest of the week at home on his own. There is another real tension here, though. The most effective way for a worship leader to get a congregation moving in worship is for him to stand up and put all he's got into worship; whether or not they join him doesn't matter, since he's away and having a great time. Yet at the same time he must fulfil a servant role for the rest of the people by being attentive to God and to them and by concentrating on his singing, playing, communication and so on. So he may need to sacrifice some of the wholehearted personal entering into worship in order to meet the needs of the other people present. Yet at no time must he be standing on the side-lines cheering people on without playing the game himself. And if he is conscious of the sacrificial nature of the role, he must make opportunities to worship without being in charge, so that he doesn't forget how to do it freely. The most important things, though, are a heart overflowing with love and praise, a frequent entering into the presence of God devotionally, and an infectious enthusiasm both for the Lord himself and for the practice of exalting him.

9. Anointing .

Anointing is the special equipping of someone by God for a particular task. It is seen most clearly in some of the Old Testament characters, people upon whom the Spirit of the Lord came, giving them special power and authority for the task he had for them. This is perhaps the most important thing of all, not just in worship leading but in any area of ministry. You may be a highly trained and theologically equipped minister, with all the skills in the world, more presence than Superman, a voice like Whitney Houston's or Marty Pellow's, musicianship which would put Beethoven in the shade, and a profound love for the Lord, but simply be the wrong person for the job, and therefore have no anointing from the Spirit. Or, more encouragingly, you may not have any of the right abilities, and yet be chosen and anointed by God such that you can do it anyway. Chapter 16 of 1 Samuel tells the story of the choosing of the next king of Israel, and of Samuel's natural assumption that the person who most looked the part would get it. But God had another man for the job; someone so unlikely that he didn't even turn up for the interview. Samuel anointed him, 'and from that day on the Spirit of the LORD came upon David in power' (v 13). What we need is not so much skilful worship leaders as anointed ones.

So what is this anointing, and how do you get it? It seems to be something which is purely a function of God's sovereign choice and grace. God chooses who he is going to anoint, and he then gives them the supernatural ability to carry out the task for which he has sovereignly chosen them. My own story may be helpful and encouraging in illustrating this. My first exposure to charismatic renewal left me absolutely terrified, and even after several years of experience within it I felt very uncomfortable indeed during worship. I was the sort of person who would be the only one in the meeting without my arms in the air because I didn't want to look unusual. Even now I'm not the most liberated of worshippers; I find jumping up and down on the spot very difficult, although fortunately that's not too much of a disadvantage in the Church of England. I probably also need inner healing for the one occasion when I didn't manage to resist the pressure from up front and joined in the dancing, only to twist my ankle so severely that I spent a couple of weeks in plaster. The ironic thing was that the song to which I was dancing contained the line 'And in his presence all our problems disappear'. I had quite a lot of time to ponder the theology of that one!

But after going to Spring Harvest for the first time, I caught a vision of what worship could be like, and became determined to do something about it. Around this time my vicar and I decided to start a second evening service as an alternative to the 1662 Choral Evensong which we held at 6.30 pm, so it seemed like an ideal opportunity to introduce some 'charismatic'-type worship. We made all the plans, bought some copies of a song-sheet with all the right stuff on it, and tuned the church piano, when all of a sudden a shocking realisation hit me with the force of a sledge-hammer – someone was going to have to lead the worship. Someone from our little church in East Anglia was going to have to stand up in front of everyone and do what Graham Kendrick and his chums did. An even worse realisation followed – it was going to have to be me. I didn't even really like charismatic worship, and now I was going to be leading it, saying things like 'Let's lift our hands to the Lord in worship,' and 'There's no need to be frightened or inhibited,' and other such things which made me squirm to hear, let alone say! I remember praying in despair (and I think it was a get-out sort of prayer, not a genuine request for help), 'Lord, if you want me to do this, you'll have to provide everything I need, because I've got nothing to contribute at all, and I don't even want to do it.' I suppose I thought God would get really upset and call someone from

Spring Harvest to come and live in our patch, but I should have known better: that's just the sort of prayer he enjoys the most, expressing utter dependence on him. Not 'Lord I could probably pull this off; I've got what it takes, but I would appreciate it if you'd just keep an eye on things in case I need a bit of assistance,' just 'Help!' He loves that sort of prayer.

I'm not saying I'm perfect, but I believe I received something from the Lord that day which far surpassed any skills I have been able to muster or any natural abilities which may have been latent in me. It didn't happen magically overnight; I had to get my guitar out and start practising, I had to go to workshops and learn practical skills, and I had to make many, many mistakes. A lot of healing in my personality had to take place, but I did learn, and I am still learning today. But on that fateful day of my prayer, I never imagined that I would one day be writing a book about leading worship. The moral of the story is: be careful what you pray; God is not averse to taking us at our word. And don't think that if you have all the skills you therefore must be the person for the job, or that if you haven't you'll never be able to do it. Seek the Lord for his anointing. If you get it, others will soon start to tell you. It's not so much ability that counts; availability and anointing are worth far more.

So powerful can God's anointing be that I have known it even happen by mistake. We had a visit from a couple from a major church in London, and the husband, who was coming on from somewhere else, arrived after his wife had spoken on the first evening, to find me fiddling about on the keyboard, an instrument which I didn't play really, preferring the guitar. After the meeting my wife and I had some personal ministry from him, during which he said that he thought the Lord was giving me a special anointing for worship. Well, I was all for that, so off he went, enthusiastically praying for me, pouring chip-oil over my head, and receiving a picture of me with a whole bank of different keyboards, leaping about exuberantly playing and leading others. He was so excited that I just didn't feel I could step in and say 'Sorry, you've got that wrong – I play guitar!' so I let him continue, certain that God would understand. But nowadays keyboard is my main instrument, and I seldom touch my guitar any more. Something happened that day, and while I still haven't got to Grade VIII (or even Grade IV, as it happens), my playing has come on by leaps and bounds, such that I often play publicly in services. I'm not sure whether God anointed his mistake anyway or whether he did know what he was doing and had a keyboard-playing future for me all along, but it was for me another lesson in the power of prayer.

Does this job spec sound a tall order? Don't despair; the Lord loves to work with people who are on the way rather than those who've arrived. I've not met the perfect worship leader yet; if you find him, let me know quickly, because he ought to be writing this, not me.

5

The Raw Materials

Having looked at the worship leader, let's move on now to see what he or she has to work with. What are some of the ingredients which go together to make a worship service, and how can we make the best of them? I've managed to identify thirteen different ingredients, some of them subdivided. Let me begin simply by explaining what I mean by these terms.

1. Liturgy

We have already attempted to define and explain this term, but for the purposes of this chapter I want to use it in its narrowest sense to mean simply material which is set to be used in the service. The most common material which I'll refer to will of course be the set prayers, creeds, canticles, lections and so on which make up the various rites used in Anglican-type worship, and which are printed out in official denominational prayer books. But non-printed material can also be liturgical. Any ceremonial which we use (this need not conjure up pictures of an Anglo-Catholic High Mass; any physical movement which we make during services, even bringing the offering plates to the front, is strictly speaking ceremonial), or any words which, though not written down, are a regular part of our worship week by week, would be included under the heading of liturgy.

2. Rubric

This word comes from the Latin for 'red', and it refers to those parts printed in red in the old Roman Catholic service books. They were simply instructions about what to do next or how to do it. Anglicans will be familiar with them as 'bluebrics' since they are now printed in blue in some of the official books. I want to adapt this word to mean anything not printed in the set liturgies which we say in order to help people through the service. This might range from very simple commands like 'Please be seated' or 'Let us pray' through to more extensive suggestions like 'Let's spend a few moments in silence before we join in the confession, to allow the Holy Spirit to bring to mind any particular things for which we need to ask God's forgiveness.' Lest Free Church readers think that rubric and liturgy are things which don't affect them, they need to be aware that there is a great tendency in non-liturgical worship (and sometimes in liturgical too) to do a transforming act whereby rubric becomes liturgy. In the Baptist church I used to attend, you could rely on one thing in particular in the service: the way in which the notices were started. Week in, week out the secretary would stand up and say, 'We do extend a very warm welcome to all in church this morning/evening, especially any visiting friends.' Secretaries came and went, they had weeks off through illness or holidays, stand-ins were found, but the words were the same. If that isn't liturgy, I don't know what is! This tendency to fossilise rubric into liturgy besets all of us who lead worship. We must fight it at all costs, and find different ways of communicating what is essentially the same information each week.

3. Notices

Sometimes it is very difficult to feel that the notices are part
of worship; they seem rather to be a break from it or an
intrusion into it. But as the worshipping community comes
together, practical details of its shared life should be given.
There are three rules here: decide where to have the notices,
give them out as creatively as you can, and keep them as
short as you can. I have experienced four different placings
for notices: right at the beginning or even before the service
starts, at the start of the sermon, at some other point in the
service, or right at the end. You will know which is the best
placing for your service. Personally I prefer them right at
the start, though that does have the disadvantage in our
church that only about thirty per cent of the congregation
hear them since most people seem to like to arrive during
the first hymn. Dealing with them creatively might involve
humour; people might actually look forward to the notices
if they know how entertaining they will be. The added
advantage of this approach is that people are far more likely
to remember what they've heard if they enjoyed hearing it.

Another thing we try to do is involve the congregation in
things in which they are not naturally involved. During
July, for example, Anglicans have to sit through up to
twenty or so sets of banns of marriage. I often remind the
congregation that these people are not just names on a list,
but real individuals about to take an incredibly important
step in life. They need our prayers, so as I'm reading the
list, why not pray for them? People will often latch on to
one or two couples whom they know personally, or who
live in their street, or who have the funniest middle names,
and pray for them, not only then but perhaps during the
week too.

Even with creativity, brevity is still important, so do all
you can to be crisp and efficient in notice-giving. Many
busy churches now print out some kind of notice sheet or

bulletin. This is often a good idea, as long as you don't then go and read the whole thing out as well. One final suggestion: why not try to find someone in the church who might have a real gift for notice-giving? I'm serious – someone who is good with words, has a quick wit and pleasant personality, and who will come over well not just to the congregation but also to any visiting friends. Perhaps Anglicans could learn from many non-conformist churches which, like my Baptist church, have a secretary whose job it is to give the notices. There might be a real ministry there for someone.

I've gone into notices here at some length, because they won't get another mention anywhere else in the book. They do need care though if they are to take their proper place in worship. I well remember one service of an hour's duration when the notices took twenty minutes. I think we'd all agree that that wasn't an ideal state of affairs.

4. The offering

Not every service will include the taking up of a money offering, and not every church will do it in the same way, but if it is done, it ought to be seen as an important part of our giving to the Lord in the context of giving ourselves to him in worship. So whether we actually take up a collection, during a hymn or as part of the service in its own right, or simply have a plate at the door which is then brought up as part of an offertory procession, we have a potentially powerful visual aid which expresses some important things about the whole nature of worship. The only thing we have to be careful to avoid, for the sake of visitors, is giving undue emphasis to this part of the service, otherwise we might reinforce in them the commonly held view that the church is only after people's money. At carol services and other special occasions where we know there are likely to be plenty of visitors, we often specifically earmark the cash collection for a charity such as Christian Aid; asking people to give to something like that, particularly at Christmas, seems much less offensive than expecting them to give to 'the church'. And at other times it can be helpful to let visitors know that we don't expect them to put anything in, and to tell them they can 'have this one on us'. People generally like that idea very much.

5. Prayer

By this I mean those times in the service when we address God directly. Obviously there are many subdivisions in this category. Prayer can be silent or vocalised; it can be aided by things to look at, music to listen to, and even incense to smell. If vocalised, that can be done by the leader alone, by members of the congregation individually, or by leader and congregation together, either from a book, or from memory (for example, the Lord's Prayer or the Grace). We will look at prayer in a little bit more detail in Chapter 8.

6. Preaching

In many churches the sermon is the *bête noire* of the service, but it can and should be a very important part of what happens when God's people come together. Through preaching we are instructed in our faith, we increase our knowledge, understanding and, hopefully, our living out of the Bible. We are challenged or comforted according to what we most need and, at times, we hear the very voice of God speaking directly into our situation. John Stott, defending the role of preaching in worship, believes

> that nothing is better calculated to restore health and vitality to the Church, or to lead its members into maturity in Christ than a recovery of true, biblical, contemporary preaching.[1]

It would be very dangerous indeed if, in a renewed church which placed all its emphasis on singing, dancing and spiritual gifts, we lost sight of the absolute necessity of the preaching and teaching ministry.

This is not a book on preaching, so purists must forgive me for including under that title any activities during the service designed to teach or apply God's word. Drama, dialogue, interviews of some sort, audio-visual aids and even videos are increasingly being used in worship, and I would want to include them here. I must add my own personal conviction that these things, while extremely useful, can never and should never replace the straight-forward preaching of God's word by a gifted and anointed preacher.

7. Response

I have written elsewhere about this, so I won't dwell on it here, but it always upsets me that the expectation implicit in the shape of the Anglican Communion Service is that once people have heard the word of God read and expounded, and had it applied to their hearts by the power of the Holy Spirit, they will immediately be filled with a burning desire to leap to their feet and recite the Creed! If we really do believe in a God who speaks to us, surely we ought to build in to our worship some ways of giving quality time to listening, and then to take notice of what he has said. I've suggested some ways we might help this to happen, as well as arguing that it should happen, in my *Responding to Preaching*.[2]

8. Testimony

For many years of my own Christian experience, the only thing God did was convert people. At least, that's the impression you got if you listened to what people talked about. Whenever anyone 'gave their testimony', it was a story about how they'd lived a life of sin and degradation, plumbing all the depths of human evil and filth, until they met the Lord at the age of twelve and now were saved and on their way to heaven. Everyone listened intently while they whipped through their catalogue of sins, but switched off when Jesus came along and rather disappointingly cleaned things up for them.

I do not in any way want to play down the glorious reality of what the saving power of Jesus can achieve, but it is true to say that we haven't always been at our most helpful in the ways in which we've shared it with others. Nevertheless, testimony is an important part of our worship, and should be increasingly so as we move more and more into times when we expect God to be among us doing things. No longer are we restricted to telling about what God did when he saved us forty-three years ago; now we have a living relationship in which we meet with God daily and often dramatically. There is much to share in terms of healing, empowering, our witness in power evangelism and so on. Again, I'm not saying that these things never happened in the past, but it does seem that God is anointing his people in a tremendous way at the moment, and in a way which means that we experience him doing all sorts of things. So what better place to share our experience of God than when we gather for worship?

A powerful testimony, given honestly, coherently and humbly, can give a real boost to our faith and expectation of God. I can remember a meeting where I was just about to start the worship time when someone asked if they could 'just give a notice'. I agreed, slightly reluctantly, but was thrilled when the notice turned out to be about someone healed of a very serious illness as a result of prayer at the last meeting. You could actually feel the faith level rise, and as we went straight into the first song, people were away in praise and gratitude to the living God who still is pleased to work among us today.

We build testimony into one of our regular services with something which we call 'mike time'. The service leader asks the congregation 'What has God been or done for you this week such that you've come along tonight to worship him?' and hands round a radio mike (it can work with a normal one if you've got a long enough lead) for anyone who wants to to speak out publicly. The contributions have varied, of course, but at times there has been a really exciting and encouraging story which has brought the congregation to spontaneous applause of the God who works so powerfully. Just this last week a teacher who has felt God calling her to begin a sort of Christian Union at her school, and who has shared testimony and asked for prayer before, announced that she had spent an away day with the children and seen twenty-four of them make a commitment to Jesus in one session. That kind of news needs sharing, and it really did affect the rest of the service. And lest this smacks of guilt-producing triumphalism, our experience is that people ask for prayer in weakness almost as often as they share victories, in spite of the way the initial question is phrased.

9. Music

To many people music is synonymous with worship. It has the power to lift our spirits to God, inspire our praise and adoration, and at times break us down in tears. Worship without music is possible, but it is difficult. Much of this book will deal with the skills needed in leading musical worship, whether by an individual, a worship group, a choir and organist, or simply your own wonderful voice. I want to identify six different types of music in worship, all of which are self-explanatory. They are hymns, what I would loosely call 'choruses' or 'worship songs', liturgical elements (for example sung settings of the *Gloria* and

Sanctus), music 'performed' rather than for congregational participation, ambient or background music and finally 'singing in the Spirit'. Each of these types requires something different from those involved, and they will be dealt with in more detail in subsequent chapters.

10. Spiritual gifts

Many of the gifts listed in the New Testament – tongues, interpretation, prophecy, discernment, healing – are to be seen most often in the context of worship. However, we must remember David Pytches' dictum that 'the meeting place is the learning place for the market place'. In other words, spiritual gifts are really for use in our evangelism out in the world, although we should still expect them to be manifested when we meet together in Jesus' name. The leader has a threefold role here: he needs to lead and encourage others by his example, he needs to test and deal with what is less than the best, and he needs to know how to help the congregation respond to what the Lord is saying or doing. The larger the congregation the harder it will be for anyone to risk giving a prophecy or anything else, so there is a real need for leadership in which the congregation feels secure and safe.

11. Silence

There is an interesting reaction going on in Christian circles: the more noisy and exuberant and dramatic charismatic worship becomes, the more people become interested in gentler alternatives such as Taizé and Celtic worship or contemplative prayer. There is even a reaction in mainstream charismatic circles against the rather hi-tech and inaccessible 'rock concert' model of conference worship bands and a swing towards 'unplugged' worship (a swing perhaps following that in the secular rock scene).

Even in churches where people apparently long for more silence in the services, it is often the case that when the leader tries to create some, people can't cope with it and feel the need to fill the space we've created with 'a scripture the Lord's given me', i.e. Psalm 119:76-132, or something similar. The current Anglican Communion liturgy specifically allows for silence to be kept in nine different places during the service, but gives no indication as to how to use it, so I have experienced very few places where any use at all is made of it.

In a world where the noise around us is increasing, we need to help congregations find and use silence. And in a world where we separate ourselves continually from one another, we need to help people towards the thrilling experience of shared silence. I suppose the ultimate in worldliness in this area is the Walkman which enables us to shut ourselves in with our own personal noise. I once taught a healing course and noticed one of the men sitting throughout with a Walkman on; it turned out he was listening to John Wimber teaching tapes (I bet nobody goes to the Vineyard and listens to tapes of me!). What we need, certainly in my church, is not so much silence which, although difficult to achieve, is just about possible, but stillness, which is next to impossible. It reflects the frenetic pace of the life we're used to that we find stillness so hard. We need to give people permission in worship by saying, as it were, 'Don't just do something; sit there!'

12. Ministry

In our church we offer prayer for healing at most of our services, and although some of it goes on after the service has ended, we still see it as part of our ministry to the Lord that we minister to each other. I won't say much about it, since it isn't the main purpose of this book, but if we really are going to understand the worship in our churches as providing God with the opportunity to come and reign among us, we will need people skilled in ministry, in recognising the Spirit's touch on people, and in prayer for healing, inner healing and deliverance.

This area has been highlighted over the past few years by the advent of the so-called 'Toronto blessing', which has taken ministry into a whole new dimension. Whether or not it is appropriate for every church to set up ministry sessions just for people to receive this anointing, it is clearly the case that the whole profile of ministry in the context of worship has been raised, and that new skills may be required. Whether or not we like it, it seems to be a fact that more people are falling over when prayed for, so some kind of precaution does need to be taken for their safety.

It is true that God often intervenes sovereignly in people's lives and works a miracle without any specific prayer or ministry having taken place, but it is nevertheless observably true that more people are healed or touched by God when there is a competent ministry team in action than when we simply 'leave it up to the Lord'. I'm sure that is because God enjoys co-operating with us in what he wants to do. I often wish that were not the case, but I'm certain it is. One of the things I enjoy doing very much is washing my car (no I won't come and do yours too!). Nowadays I usually do it alone, and I make sure I do it regularly every year, whether it needs doing or not. But when our boys were younger, it used to be a regular family occasion. We'd put on wellies and coats, grab our sponges, and attack the grime with great enthusiasm. However, as is often the case with young children, Steve and Paul's enthusiasm soon got diverted elsewhere. Before long they would decide that the pavement was much dirtier than the car, so they'd give that a good wipe over. Then they'd remember that it was the car they were supposed to be washing, so the sponges would go straight back onto the bodywork. They'd then decide to wash the flowerbeds in the front garden, and again the accumulated soil on the sponges was transferred back to the car. This went on until finally the job was finished and we'd all get into the car, go down to the local garage, pay £1.75 and go through the car-wash. Why did I do it? And why does God choose to work with us when he could do things so much more quickly and efficiently when we are off somewhere else? I did it because I loved (and still love) seeing my boys enjoying themselves helping me. I'd rather spend the time with them inefficiently than do it on my own with much less mess. In short, I value the relationships more than I value efficiency.

God is the same. I often wish he were not, but I believe he is. He has chosen to set this world up as a partnership; just as he asked for Adam and Eve's co-operation in Eden he invites ours now. I don't think it is without significance that so many of Jesus' parables about the kingdom were taken from the farming world; the partnership of human sowing, tending and reaping with divine life and growth seems to be a perfect picture of a kingdom which is brought in sovereignly by God, but as a result of his people praying 'your kingdom come'.

Thus if we are to work in the correct partnership with God we must take our responsibilities seriously. Particularly in the area of healing and ministry we need to train to become proficient in praying for those with whom God is working in healing power. We have taken on John Wimber's model and praxis for healing at our church, but whatever model you use, make sure you do use it. If your worship goes as you hope it will, you'll need to.

13. One another!

This ingredient isn't quite in the same league as the others, but it needs to be mentioned since it is increasingly being given liturgical significance, and not only in liturgical churches. In the past, worship was often seen as a very individualistic and private matter. Anglicans, certainly, spoke of 'making my Communion', and in most branches of the Church one regarded one's fellow worshippers as intruders rather than as valued companions (and often glared at them accordingly!). But now things are different.

It is my conviction that the division often found in many Anglican churches (and perhaps others too) is not primarily about age and generation, nor about traditional versus modern worship – these are merely symptoms of a deeper issue. At rock bottom, it seems to me, there is a fundamental split between those who respond to God (if they do at all) privately and secretly, with no one else being a part of that response, and those who are quite happy to 'let it all hang out' spiritually. The watershed was the church's rediscovery of the doctrine of the body of Christ in the 1970s: those whose formation was largely before then will dread the very notion of any kind of public display of their spirituality, while those brought up since then will have an understanding that we are all in this together, and that each individual has both a responsibility for and accountability to other Christians. Obviously this is more than just a generational thing. Younger people who have found faith in a church with a pre-seventies ethos will naturally be socialised into its ways, and older people who have an encounter with God later in life in a post-seventies context will be likely to take on the ways of behaving appropriately there.

As the church grows more and more 'post-seventies' in style there is much more of an emphasis on the fact that we come *together* into God's presence. Anglicans recognise this liturgically in the 'Peace', hardly the most peaceful time during the service, when everyone wanders about greeting their fellow-worshippers with anything from a polite handshake to an enthusiastic bear-hug, depending on the degree of renewal to have hit the church so far. Non-Anglicans are not slow, either, to take this up in various ways, perhaps by having the Peace without necessarily calling it that, or by looking at one another as we sing songs addressed to others rather than to God or when we say 'the Grace', or in other creative ways. One excellent song which we still use from time to time as a 'sung Peace' is from Graham Kendrick's Christmas *Make Way, The Gift*. The tune and words are very simple:

> Peace to you,
> We bless you now in the name of the Lord,
> Peace to you,
> We bless you now in the name of the Prince of Peace,
> Peace to you.

One of the most moving worship experiences I've ever had was singing this song in a crowd of 11,000 people. We sang it through a few times, and then simply began wandering around, hugging friends and strangers alike and singing to each other. In print it sounds terrifying; at the time it was truly beautiful.

This relating to one another, however we do it, is an important part of worship in the body of Christ (but then I would say that as a post-seventies Christian!). Even if we don't build it into the service itself, it will still happen before and after, so we may as well include it in the list of things involved in worship.

Here, then, are thirteen things which may make up our worship services. Maybe I haven't mentioned every last jot or tittle of the service, but these seem to me to cover most of it. How can we make the most of these ingredients and mix them together in a way which makes a mouth-watering offering for our God? I'll be looking at this in a later chapter, but it is worth saying that I wouldn't want to leave the impression that all there is to a successful worship service is good ingredients. A recipe has much more to it than a list of things to put in, even if you do choose the right ones and add them in the right order. There's a method as well, and I want to end this chapter with a brief look at it. I'll do this by changing the metaphor from cooking to smoking, and use an illustration which I hope will clarify the relationship between these ingredients, the worshippers and the service as a whole. For my illustration, I want to look at incense.

It is a well-known fact that many Anglo-Catholic, Roman and Orthodox churches (and slightly fewer Baptist and New churches) use incense in the course of their worship. However, not many people know exactly how it works. Probably not many people have much of a desire to know, but for the purposes of this analogy, I'm afraid you'll have to find out. I leave aside the vexed question of whether we *ought* to use incense (although personally I love it, and think it a great pity that they didn't have any at Toronto); I'm simply mentioning it to illustrate a point.

To be a successful thurifer (that's the person who swings it around and is otherwise generally responsible for it), you need first of all two ingredients. The first is the incense itself, which comes in small globules rather like little bits of a rather disreputable brand of demerara sugar. This is slightly smelly, but nothing to write home about as yet. The second is charcoal, which looks like a much larger version of the sort of tablets you take with you when you go on holiday to Tunisia or wherever. The idea is to put the incense on the charcoal, which then makes it give out its smoke and fragrance. But one vital thing is still missing, without which the whole exercise is futile: fire. The charcoal must first be ignited; in fact it must be blown or fanned to glowing heat before it will do anything at all to the incense.

Let me explain my analogy. It helps me to think of the worship ingredients listed above as individual grains of incense, each with their own particular fragrance to offer, but at the moment sitting there doing nothing. There is no particular delight for the Lord in a printed prayer shut between two pages of a prayer book, or a song sitting silently in a closed song book or wound round and round on a piece of magnetic tape. The ingredients need more than their own intrinsic value to turn them into worship. Secondly, I can easily imagine many worshippers as being like charcoal – dull, dusty and, like their smaller counterparts, capable of stopping anything. Even though it is a start, those two things together won't achieve much without the third: fire. For worship to be successful, the fire of the Holy Spirit needs to come and ignite the hearts of the worshippers first of all, until we are glowing hot in our love for the Lord. Then, and only then, are we capable of taking the different ingredients in the service and offering them as a gift to the Lord to rise fragrant before him, blessing him and giving him delight in his children.

I find this a helpful analogy, since it explains our responsibility in worship to be prepared and in tune with God. Churches which use incense need to light the charcoal about fifteen minutes before the service begins so that it has time to catch and grow hot. When we rush late into church more hot and bothered than on fire with the Lord, it is no wonder that our worship often fizzes, smoulders a bit and then goes out. Preparation of the worshippers is perhaps the most serious lack in worship today. We wander into the Lord's presence with little care or attention, and then blame the leaders because the worship didn't take off or because the sermon or the prayers didn't do anything for us. To go back to my analogy, the incense will only be as smelly as the heat of the charcoal allows. All the ingredients we've listed are simply means to an end; it's up to us to make the right use of them in a way which is anointed by the Spirit of God.

Notes

1 John Stott, *I Believe in Preaching* (London: Hodder & Stoughton, 1982) p 338.
2 John Leach, *Responding to Preaching* (Cambridge: Grove, 1997).

6

Planning for Worship

Planning is in some ways the most difficult stage of all in worship leading. I would want to argue that it is certainly the most important. Therefore I want to devote a whole chapter to it, since worship times can stand or fall on the work done (or not done) before they ever begin.

Who should plan? I don't think there are any set rules. Obviously it is first and foremost a matter of prayer and listening to the Lord. So it may be helpful if there is some liaison between the different people involved in the service; the preacher, the service leader and the music leader, if you have one. Try to discern together where the Lord is wanting to go with you. Some churches have a 'worship committee' or something similar which meets weekly to pray and to plan the Sunday services; in some ways this is ideal, but I have to admit to feeling at times that it is a luxury which many busy churches can't afford. It depends on how much emphasis you place on Sunday worship as opposed to the everyday work of the church; is the week to be used for making Sunday extra special for God's people, or is Sunday used for the equipping of the people for their work and witness during the rest of the week? This question, 'Where is the real church?' will have to be answered, because it will affect the amount of time you give to preparation for worship.

I want to look at the process of planning from a dual point of view: putting together a whole service, and planning a musical worship slot within that service. As a general overview of the subject I've found it helpful to think through this process by using the analogy of stringing a pearl necklace. We'll look at that analogy, and then look in more detail at the actual planning process.

1. Raw materials

We begin with the raw materials from which the necklace (or worship time) is to be constructed:

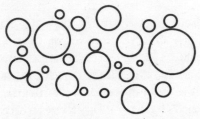

We've already talked about the raw materials for worship in the previous chapter, and the fact that simply being there doesn't make them into worship, any more than a pile of pearls is a necklace. Three more things are needed.

2. Integrity

The next thing your pearls need to begin their transformation into a necklace is a bit of string to hold them all together. This is analogous to the *integrity* of a worship service.

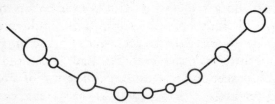

Integrity is the feeling that all the ingredients in the service are in some way linked. Most of the time this is obvious: we choose hymns which are at least vaguely to do with the theme of the service, and readings and prayers which reflect this too. But there are other more creative things we can do to make the service feel like a whole unit. Omission of some items is allowed – we don't have to use every last bit of the liturgy (written or unwritten) at every service. It can be great, at times, to omit one part and really concentrate on another which ties in with the theme much better. As long as the congregation has a balanced diet over a long period of time, it doesn't have to be fed every single nutrient at every meal. (I'll say a bit more about this, including its legality or otherwise, later.) So, for example, a service on the theme of the character of God may make a big thing of the Creed or some other statement of faith, while skipping quite quickly over the penitential section, whereas in another service where 'world mission' is the theme, we may want to do without some other bits of the liturgy in order to give more time for prayer and intercession. Similarly, the type of music we choose may vary according to what we're emphasising. We may choose to cut down our spoken prayers and give time for a real crying out to the Lord in song. Non-musical items similarly need to be thought out. There's not much you can do about the notices, but testimonies can be chosen with care to reflect God's working in an area relevant to the subject matter of the service.

I suppose the key to integrity is to have a theme for the service and to make sure that everyone knows what it is. To some this may be a radical thought; we haven't bothered with that sort of thing before, so what's the problem? The problem is that people need to feel part of something they understand in order to get the most from and give the most to worship. A seemingly random collection of hymns, prayers and readings, thrown together in a heap with no visible thread running between them, will simply confuse people and alienate them from the task in hand. And even if the hymns and prayers took you seven hours of determined prayer and preparation to throw together, it does people no good if they can't detect the obscure link which your incredibly creative but rather too complex mind has used to hold the whole thing in place. A simple sentence at the beginning of the service can let people into the secret in such a way that they rejoice in your creativity as the service unfolds rather than being baffled by it.

3. Direction

So far we have some pearls and a string to hold them together. Next we have to think about the order in which the pearls are strung.

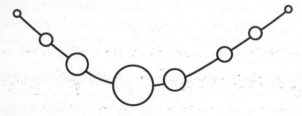

If a *theme* ensures integrity in a service, an *aim* is essential for direction. Just as the worshippers need to feel that the whole thing holds together, so they also need to feel that it is not a static unity but a dynamic one, moving from a starting point towards a clearly visible goal. The service leader needs to ask two questions: 'Where will people be starting from as they come to worship?' and 'Where do I and God want them to be by the end?' A subsidiary question, once these two have been answered, would need to be asked: 'If that's where we're moving from and to, which route will we be going along on the journey?' To think through these questions carefully in preparation is to provide some sort of map for the service which may prevent it from becoming hopelessly lost in the uncharted sea of charismatic spontaneity or compulsory liturgy. In a while we'll move on to look at this area in more detail.

4. Flow

Finally we have to make sure that the pearls on our string fit together neatly so that no bare string is showing. That's what I mean by *flow*.

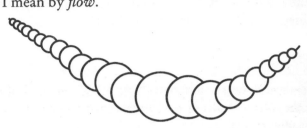

How can we make the journey in worship as smooth as possible? Our choice of items must enable the worshippers to move through the service with no bumps or bruises.

This, in outline, is how we might begin thinking about how we put the service together. Let's move on now to consider in more detail the actual planning process. We'll look at the theory, and then end with a couple of practical examples.

Tools for the job

As with any job, we begin with the tools we need. It may be possible to get things done without the right ones, but it won't be easy. So what's in the toolbox?

1. Repertoire

This is a list of all the songs/hymns/liturgy you ever use. With so much on the market it is essential to limit yourselves to those items which you know well and can use effectively. This is particularly important with worship songs, which are being churned out at a phenomenal rate. Our repertoire is a list of about 120 or so songs which we use, and which therefore excludes the other 15,000 on the market which we don't. My experience is that to choose a new song which no one knows because you like it, or even because it fits in with the theme, usually kills the worship stone dead. People can only really worship with songs they know well, so you need a carefully worked out strategy for introducing new material. We've also found it helpful *not* to rush back from Spring Harvest and begin teaching the twenty-eight new songs through which we met the Lord powerfully in the Big Top. We try to revise the repertoire about six months later, when the one or two which have lasting use for us are left and everyone's long forgotten the rest. We update our repertoire annually, and try to make sure that we lose as many songs as we put on, so that the number stays fairly constant around the 120 mark.

Isn't this terribly restricting to the Spirit? Maybe, but it's really liberating for the worship team and the congregation. In our church we're simply not competent enough as musicians just to be able to pick up and play well anything which is thrown at us, especially if this happens week after week. But we can manage a limited number of songs which we know we'll be staying with for at least a year or so; we can work on them individually and as bands, knowing that this is a good long-term investment. Similarly we recognise the fact that the congregation needs time to learn new material and relax into it enough to be able to worship through it. While some churches handle this by singing the new song thirty-five times through on its first appearance, we go about it in a slightly more subtle way than that over a longer (but less intensive) period of time. So while a repertoire does, by definition, limit the number of songs we can use, it also saves hours of time and sweat. And if it is well chosen, it needn't be as restrictive as it sounds; there should be songs to cover most moods and themes.

A hymn repertoire is very much easier to put together, and once done it will very rarely need updating. Similarly liturgy changes less frequently, and the legal options will be available through official publications.

2. Categorisation

Having a finite number of songs from which to choose your material for a particular service can save you hours of time. Some kind of a categorisation of them into different types can speed up the process even further. There are two ways of doing this: thematically and according to *feel*. Many of the songbooks contain thematic indexes so it shouldn't take much work to lift out those songs which are on your repertoire and list them according to the themes given; someone else has done most of the work for you there. But it is much less common to find categorisation according to feel done for you, so we have developed our own convention which has worked well for us. In case it might be helpful, I'll briefly describe the six different categories we use. No doubt you'll be able to provide your own examples from music and liturgy with which you are familiar.

(i) Adoration and love. This is perhaps the most intimate expression of worship. We simply stand before God, look him straight in the eye, and tell him that we love him. As with two human beings who are in love, it is an emotional rather than a rational experience. Although theological verbalisation is at a minimum, and in one sense it is a whispering of 'sweet nothings' in God's ear, our profound love for him is far from being a 'nothing'. Rather adoration is the highest point of that relationship with God which gives all theology its meaning, although it may be beyond theological expression. This kind of worship is commanded by God: 'Love the LORD your God with all your heart and with all your soul and with all your strength' (Deut 6:5);

celebrated throughout the Song of Songs (although we mustn't spiritualise the primary meaning of this book, a celebration of human erotic love); and enjoyed by several of the psalmists, for example in Psalms 18:1, 42:1–2, 73:25, 84:2 and 116:1. Whether we reach it during a quiet part of a worship slot, in a moment of profound stillness during silent contemplation, or at a climactic point in a service such as the *Sanctus* or the moment of receiving Communion, this most intimate place really is the 'Holy of Holies' where we meet God in a depth of relationship quite out of the ordinary. We may meet God in quiet intimacy, such as that reflected by Simeon in the *Nunc Dimittis*, or in awe and reverence, as Isaiah did in the Temple (Is 6), or in a mixture of both, as expressed by Mary in the *Magnificat*.

Similarly, the sort of music which is appropriate here can be soft and gentle, or occasionally strong and majestic. Hymns are slightly less helpful in this mood, because they tend to be too wordy and theologically complex, and are often sung about God rather than to him, but there are nevertheless some contenders. While simplicity in surroundings may speak of intimacy with God, a sense of awe and reverence can be heightened by rich banners and vestments, incense and dramatic ceremonial. Worship seldom begins in this experience of intimate love, but it should often arrive there.

(ii) Celebration and joy. This is a slightly less profound but much more exuberant form of worship, which might be described without undue reverence as having a spiritual knees-up in the Lord's presence. Their traditional reserve makes this type of worship slightly more difficult for Anglicans, but New Church people love it. Leaping, clapping, dancing and shouting before God – everyone has a really good time enjoying themselves, enjoying God and letting him enjoy them. There need be nothing irreverent about this type of worship; I believe God loves seeing his

children having a good time just as much as I do mine. The impression one gets of God's people in the Old Testament is that they frequently indulged in such exuberant worship. When they brought the ark to Jerusalem, David and the whole house of Israel celebrated 'with all their might before the LORD', with singing and all sorts of musical instruments (2 Sam 6:5), and after the return from the exile in Babylon, the restored community have such a good time of worship at the dedication ceremony for the walls of Jerusalem that 'the sound of rejoicing... could be heard far away' (Neh 12:27–43). Many of the Psalms seem to reflect this type of worship, especially the Hallelujah Psalms (Ps 146 – 150), as do some of the canticles used in liturgical worship. In the Eucharist we celebrate with the offertory sentence 'Yours Lord is the greatness', and many hymns and songs would provide musical accompaniment appropriate to this mood. Major festivals lend themselves to celebration, and flowers, banners, dance and an unrestrained dose of the Peace can add considerably to the sense of celebration.

(iii) Proclamation and witness. Our hope as Christians is that quite apart from doing us good, worship can have an effect on those currently outside the kingdom. Sometimes we can design it specifically to do so. Many songs announce the character and deeds of God, not just so that we can celebrate them but in order to draw others into an awareness of him. Sometimes we address God directly, so that others are somehow caught up in our worship, while in other songs the words may express our corporate response to God, having a function similar to that of the liturgical creeds and acclamations. Sometimes our words are addressed directly to the outsiders, as we challenge them to see our God being worshipped and to join in. Much of the 'March for Jesus' material has this aim.

Old Testament passages like 1 Chronicles 29:10–20, where David praises the Lord for his provision for the building of the Temple, provide good examples of the drawing of others into worship, as do many of the Psalms, notably Psalms 95 to 100, three of which have found their way into Anglican liturgical worship as the *Venite* (Ps 95), the *Cantate Domino* (Ps 98) and the *Jubilate* (Ps 100). Revelation 19:1–9 provides a New Testament example of the saints and angels in heaven being drawn into the worship of God and the Lamb, and many of the evangelical 'mission' hymns (such as 'Blessed assurance, Jesus is mine') attempt to speak to outsiders.

(iv) Declaration and warfare. Sometimes we may feel in worship that instead of proclamation to people we have moved into declaration to the Enemy. My dictionary didn't help me much with the difference between these two concepts: to 'proclaim' means 'to declare...' and to 'declare' means 'to proclaim...'. But I certainly know what it feels like when I'm worshipping. Sometimes when we approach God in worship it is as if he invites us to come and stand where he stands, and then shows us the world or different situations through his eyes. This can often fill one not just with heartfelt compassion, but also with a real sense of outrage and righteous indignation. If you've never had this experience, pray for it; I believe it's right from time to time to share our Father's anger at the destruction and havoc wrought on his world by the Enemy. The Greek word translated 'rebuke', used throughout the Gospels for Jesus' reaction to sickness, evil spirits, storms and so on, reflects this sense of anger at the trouble caused by Satan. We too must know this sort of sanctified anger, and be able to express it and minister to others through it.

A famous passage in 2 Chronicles 20 describes how King Jehoshaphat, faced with rather a difficult battle, decides to send out a group of singers before the troops to worship the Lord. There is some evidence that the Hebrew here could mean that the singers were 'in splendid array', an exegesis which has led some scholars to suggest that they were in fact the robed choir. Far be it from me to suggest that this is a scriptural warrant for dealing drastically with recalcitrant church musicians; in any case it didn't do the King any good because during the worship God came and finished off the enemy. No more Ammonites and Moabites, but he still had his choir!

We need of course to be careful that we don't overstep the mark and become too obsessed with the Enemy when we should be concentrating on God. Like the Archangel Michael in Jude 9 we mustn't take it on ourselves to enter single-handedly into battle against Satan. It seems to me that in the Bible it is the Lord who rebukes Satan, although believers can and should be involved in the rebuking and expulsion of lesser demons who are affecting people and places. But the sense of anger and outrage which calls on Jesus himself to march out against evil is something which we can bring to our worship, and which has a rightful place there. Many hymns and songs express this feel, although the Anglican liturgy is a bit too 'nice' to get into any real conflict.

(v) Intercession and penitence. When I first put together this material on different types of worship, I stopped at the four we've dealt with so far. I had interceded, of course, and I'd even been penitent on occasions, but none of it really felt much like worship. But now I'm becoming more and more convinced that these things have a place when we meet corporately, and indeed will become increasingly important as we move on in time. One of the most powerful songs written recently, and one of the few which I believe will stand the test of time and still be powerful many years from now, is 'Restore, O Lord, the honour of Your name'.

There was a time in charismatic circles when this was just about the only song of its kind, calling on God for a fresh dose of his renewing and reviving power not just for the church but also for the world. But there has been a sea-change and more and more current songs have this kind of mood. I remember in my first parish, a rather Anglo-Catholic one where we used to follow strictly the Church's liturgical calendar (a practice, I have argued, from which other churches could benefit greatly), remarking to a friend while trying to choose music for services during Lent, 'When is someone going to start writing some miserable charismatic songs?' Heartfelt penitence is, of course, an experience which is far from being miserable, but the element of sorrow and brokenness seems to have been restored to much contemporary charismatic worship. I see it as a real sign of the maturity of renewal that we have at last come to the place where our intimate celebration of the glory of God has brought us to the point of needing to say 'Woe is me!'

(vi) Teaching songs. Finally we recognise this category which, while not strictly speaking 'worship' nevertheless does have a place within our repertoire, and is especially important for children. Songwriters like Ishmael have specialised in this genre, and we have found many of his songs helpful in our children's ministry (and occasionally in church), though we try to distinguish clearly for the benefit of the congregation between them and worship.

I wouldn't like to say that every last song, hymn or liturgical text will fit neatly into one of these six categories, but I do find this sort of classification a helpful tool in understanding what's going on in a worship time, and in planning for worship.

The process

Having assembled our tools, let's get to work. I find it useful to think of the planning process as one which has five distinct stages which need to be worked through methodically. I begin with the *context*, and then move through the *feel*, *aim* and *flow*, and then onto the *content*.

The great temptation, of course, is to begin with the content. After all, the question burning in our minds as we come to plan is 'What are we going to sing/say?', and the urgency of the question can make us want to rush on to think up some good songs or hymns. But I want to argue strongly that there is a considerable amount of work to be done before we get anywhere near that stage. So let's examine each stage of the process in turn.

1. Context

I don't want to make this all too complicated, but I find it helpful to subdivide this heading into three. We need to examine the *thematic context*, the *liturgical context*, and the *congregational context*. So first we need to begin asking some of these questions: What is the theme of the service? What decides this; a preaching series, a lectionary, the church calendar, the leader's whim, or what? Where is the church at the moment; what does the Lord seem to be concentrating on with you?

Secondly, what is the liturgical context? Is it a Communion service, an unstructured Rave, a Service of the Word, an ecumenical celebration? The possibilities are endless, but the overall shape will obviously affect the planning considerably.

Finally, who is likely to be there? How many might there be; where will they be (if anywhere) in their Christian pilgrimage? Are there any events which have happened recently which may affect the way people are feeling (like the Hillsborough disaster we've already mentioned)? What will be the corporate mood of those present?

Even the sex of those present may be an important consideration. Once several years ago I was asked to lead some worship at our Anglican clergy chapter meeting. I chose some songs and began, but we were only halfway through the first before I realised that I had planned a disaster. I had chosen several Vineyard-type songs where men's and women's voices echoed each other, and here I was, long before the ordination of women, in a group of eleven men and one deaconess who happened to have laryngitis. It did not go well! More careful planning might have warned me about this so that I could have handled the slot differently.

Answers to all these questions can help to put your worship into context, so that it has an appropriate framework and fits in with where people are at. Experience will help you to be able to answer at least some of them fairly easily, and the insights of other people may be helpful too. When you think you've got a good understanding of this, move on to think about the next stage.

2. Feel

Having decided the context and theme of the service, spend some time getting inside it. Ask yourself particularly what the people will feel like being there. If you're planning a specific music slot within a service, take this a bit further by asking what they might feel like by the time they reach that part. If it comes after a sermon all about sin, hell and eternal punishment, they may not feel too keen on joining in vigorously with something from the adoration list. Similarly songs of deep penitence may not reflect exactly the mood of the congregation directly after a church family baptism. Think yourself into the situation, and try to get in touch with it on an emotional level too.

3. Aim

The *feel* is very much about where people will be starting from as they move into worship; the *aim* is about where you want them to be by the time you stop. It's one thing to give people permission to be where they are, but to do nothing about moving them on from there is quite another. If your desire in leading worship is to bring people into the presence of God, with the expectation that he will encounter them, it is clear that there certainly ought to be some change in the way people feel as a result. God may, of course, have other ideas entirely, but it never hurts to have an aim in mind, since it is a great help in actually getting somewhere rather than running on the spot. So, for example, people may feel very penitent and unworthy after the hellfire sermon, but it would be good if we could lead them towards a place of forgiveness, peace and security. Similarly great excitement and exuberance are fine, but people may benefit from being led more deeply into the worship and adoration of their God.

4. Flow

Knowing where you're starting from and where you're hoping to get to are very useful prerequisites for any journey, but there is one more thing that you need: some idea of the route to be taken. That's what I mean by the flow of the worship. Returning to the categories of worship I mentioned before, you need to decide how you are going to use those categories to put together a service or slot which will move people from the feel they have now to the aim which we have for them. So, for example, how are you actually going to get from putting the fear of God into people to helping them to feel secure and accepted by him? Theologically we would be able to answer that: we'd need to move through an acknowledgement of our own sin, an affirmation of God's grace in forgiveness, penitence, reception of forgiveness, and celebration of freedom. So can we do that in the context of worship? Yes, we can.

I find it helpful to try and draw a 'graph' of how I expect a worship time might go, in order to get the flow right. The most useful way to do this is to plot exuberance against time, so that, for example, a move from noisy celebration towards quiet intimacy and adoration would look like this:

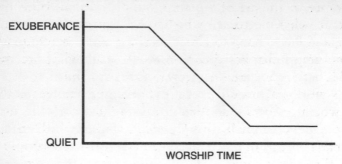

A worship slot which built up from the quietness of, for example, the administration of Communion to an enthusiastic time of warfare might be represented like this:

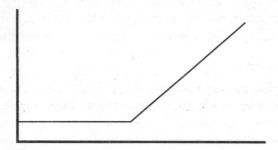

This sort of graph might describe celebration which quietened down into penitence, and then moved into a declaration of God's forgiving power and his victory over sin:

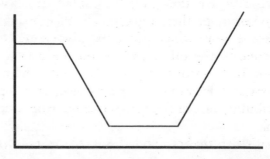

You might find all this a bit too mathematical, and of little relevance to the art of worship, but I find it helpful. Not least, it helps me to see whether my expectations are too high, and I am trying to cram too much into a worship slot. If the graph changes direction more than twice, we may well lose the congregation around the next bend!

It's worth mentioning here that although the idea is that the worship flows smoothly from one phase to the next, there can occasionally be great impact in a sudden and dramatic change of direction. The most obvious example of this I've experienced was when, after a couple of increasingly rousing choruses of 'Majesty', we were suddenly dropped right into a very quiet arrangement of 'You laid aside your majesty'. The starkness of the contrast spoke volumes to me about Jesus' self-emptying. This is the very antithesis of 'flow', and can only be used very rarely. We call it 'contraflow'.

5. Content

Finally, having thought through the context, feel, aim and flow, you can begin to plan the contents. We've noted that it's very tempting to begin here, but unless it is the culmination of the process outlined above, it may well be haphazard, to say the very least. But now that you know exactly where you're going, you can choose material which will work together to take you there, by the route you've decided on. Find some songs or liturgy which pick people up from where they are, find some more which reflect where you hope they'll get to, and then, most importantly, find some more which can act as pivot songs to help move from one to the other. Decide on the points where some spoken interjections might help, and where you might appropriately leave some air-holes and open up for contributions from the congregation, prophetic words, and so on.

That's the theory. You don't, of course, have to do it

exactly like that, but I've set it out in order to show you
how to do it if you do want to use that framework, or to
show you how a similar framework which felt more
appropriate for you might be worked out. But I do regard
learning to plan as a little bit like learning to drive. When
you're used to it you can break all the rules with impunity,
but in order to pass your test you do have to know what
the rules are, and stick to them, at least for a while. So why
not try working through this process exactly by the book?
After a couple of months (or years, depending how quick
on the uptake you are), you may want to spread your wings
and try other ways of working, but only once this model is
firmly under your skin. And of course the other advantage
of it is that being in some ways so rigid makes it easily
transferable. I have trained many people in its use, and it
does seem to be the case that most of them have got hold of
it pretty quickly.

At this point, some of you with a leaning towards a more
spontaneous approach might be feeling that this whole
thing seems so sewn up that it would be impossible for God
to come and do anything. There is indeed a danger in this
approach that having picked a list of songs we can do
nothing but bash through them regardless of what's going
on around us. Two things need to be said about this. The
first is that there is no merit in flexibility for the sake of it.
If we really have chosen our songs both thoughtfully and
prayerfully, seeking to discern in advance what God is
wanting to do, there should be no need to change things as
we go along. If we find ourselves constantly being thrown
by the Spirit during worship, and feeling the need to go off
in completely unplanned directions, we may need to look
again at the way in which we prepare. Having said that,
however, we do need to be free to be able to change if the
need arises. How can we do that?

One possible answer is to have a list which begins with
three or four songs, and which then branches into several

different strands. So after a general start with a few call-to-worship or celebratory songs, we might have three alternative lists – one based around adoration, one continuing the celebration, and one perhaps moving into penitence. It's up to the worship leader to choose the list which feels most appropriate when you all get there. This obviously requires a lot of preparation on the part of the musicians, and will involve the frustration of never using two-thirds of what you practise, but it is a good way of keeping built-in flexibility.

Another, perhaps better, way is to have a strategy for coping with spontaneity. We'll talk about this paradoxical-sounding concept later, but careful musical preparation can mean that whatever happens you can cope, and cope in a way which leaves the congregation feeling that you'd planned to do it that way all along! What really allows good flexibility is a firm grasp of the material and good personal relationships; you really can get to the point where you know the musicians so well that you'll all spontaneously start exactly the same song at the right time. You learn to know how others think, and they know how you're thinking, so you sort of 'feel' your way through difficult moments.

Let me end this section with a word on the place of prayer. I've concentrated very heavily on the human side of the planning process, but you mustn't take that to mean that it's the most important bit. In the last analysis, we want to choose the songs, hymns and prayers which God knows will bless him and the congregation the most. I believe he longs to communicate with us, and will give us some clues about how a meeting or service is going to go, so that we can aid what he wants to do, rather than get in the way. Very often when I'm praying I suddenly find myself singing in my head a song or progression of songs which would be just right for the service I'm planning, even if that isn't specifically what I'm praying about. So make prayer a priority, on your own, and with others involved. The Enemy will do all he can to prevent this, and the sad thing is that the worship slot can often go well without prayer. If that weren't true it'd be easier, because we'd know that if we didn't pray it would flop, so we'd make sure we did pray, at the very least to save ourselves embarrassment. But it isn't like that; things can go very well (or appear to) and so we feel the need for prayer less, not more. However, I believe this is false thinking, and sooner or later it is all bound to catch up with us, as the spiritual poverty of the worship we're leading becomes apparent to us and probably to others too. So pray first, then plan. Either without the other is a recipe for disaster, but both together will mean that you have done your very best for the congregation and for the Lord.

7

Using Liturgy

We have already looked in some detail at the subject of liturgy: what it is, where we got it from, and how important it is, especially for churches moving in the new things which the Holy Spirit is doing. You will have noticed the fact that I am an ardent lover of liturgical worship, and believe that it provides the best framework of all for freedom in the Spirit and spontaneity in responding to him. You can imagine, therefore, how deeply it upsets me when I find Anglican churches where there is a profound ignorance of the principles behind liturgy, and where it is regarded at the very best as a necessary evil, and where no care is given either to using it effectively or to training others to get the most out of it. This chapter is offered in an attempt to get some leaders of liturgical churches to rediscover this most tremendous resource and to renew it, along with other areas of their churches' life, so that it becomes a means through which the Holy Spirit may flow in his invigorating power. I write not just to clergy, but to all who have responsibility for leading others in liturgical worship, and also to those whose privilege it is week by week to join in with the forms of worship which have been used by God's people in one way or another for many hundreds of years. If non-Anglican readers want to skip this bit you may, but if you

131

do stick with it you might gain some insight into the effective use of this rich resource. I simply want to make six suggestions about how to approach liturgy.

1. Respect it!

While the average Anglican may firmly believe that the ASB plopped suddenly out of the sky one November morning in 1980, the truth is that it was part of a long process stretching back for centuries; a process which is being continued forward into the future. The Church has been seeking the best ways to formulate its public worship down the years, and a tremendous amount of hard work and prayer has gone into the evolution of the liturgy we now use. The creativity of scholars and poets, some no doubt more and some less devout than others, the doctrinal sharpening up of truth by theologians, the discussions and disagreements which have been resolved into consensus: all these have left us the legacy through which we can now meet God in worship. Since 1980 many more Anglican liturgical texts have been added to our resource stock, and now that the ASB is nearing the end of its life, the process goes on once more in preparation for the new millennium. We have already mentioned the need to see ourselves in historical and geographical continuity with the body of Christ through space and time. Our liturgy, and its constant updating, can help to remind us of our heritage and our brotherhood with other Christians around the world.

Having said a little about the formation of the ASB in the run-up to 1980, the Church of England Liturgical Commission (which was responsible for its publication) offered it humbly to the Church with these words:

> Those who use [the words of this book] do well to recognise their transience and imperfection; to treat them as a ladder, not a goal; to acknowledge their power in shaping faith and

kindling devotion, without claiming that they are fully adequate to the task. Only the grace of God can make up what is lacking in the faltering words of men. It is in reliance on such grace that this book is offered to the Church, in the hope that God's people may find in it a means in our day to worship Him with honest minds and thankful hearts.[1]

Those of us who have been using it for nearly two decades are only too aware of its 'transience and imperfection', but the principles behind its production are still as valid as ever.

It seems to me that this is exactly the sort of respect one should have for the liturgy; not any particular piece of liturgy necessarily, but the corporate body of material through which we worship God. Those who receive and use liturgical texts in the spirit in which they are offered will not go far wrong.

2. Learn it!

One of the first Anglican services I ever went to was a rather elaborate 'High Mass' at the local parish church. My Baptist sensibilities were offended not so much by the hordes of servers mincing around the sanctuary, nor by the candles which seemed to sprout from every available crack in the stonework, nor even by the quantity of smoke which almost totally obscured the back wall, but simply by the fact that people not only had service books, but then didn't even use them. They would shut their eyes and carry on through the service without once looking to see what was going on in the book. This just proved what I had always been taught about the Church of England, and more so: not only were they into 'vain repetition', but they were so far into it that they didn't even need books to repeat it from!

Yet now, after a twenty-five-year love affair with the Church of England (which began that day and grows daily more intense for me), I have come to see the value in learned liturgy. When the words are so deeply entrenched in our minds we are free to use them from the heart. There is no need to fumble for the right page or even hold the book; we can simply close our eyes, lift our faces to God (and our hands as well if we choose), and worship him with body, mind and spirit. Similarly, when other moods are appropriate we can be free to express our devotion physically as well as vocally, and make our bodies say what we want to say to God without demanding that they act as a personal lectern as well.

Learning the words frees not just our bodies in worship, but also our minds. Those of us who were brought up to memorise Scripture know how deeply it penetrated into our very beings by the frequency with which verses pop up at appropriate times, usually in the Authorised Version. Liturgy works in the same way, and can be a treasure store of the grace of God, not just during public worship but at odd times during the rest of the week too. When we use the words in the course of a service, we are using something which comes not from a book but from somewhere deep within us. We have already taken it on board and digested it, so that when we use the words we are using something already dear to us, something which is already a part of our devotional lives. Yes, of course there is a danger of vain, mindless repetition, but in my experience this is far more frequently a product of vain, mindless worshippers than of the liturgy itself. Learn the liturgy and encourage others to do so too. You'll notice the difference in the feel of your worship very quickly.

If your charismatic sensibilities are offended by this advice, might I remind you that this is exactly how worship songs work? The words may be there, on the screen or in the songbook, but most seasoned worshippers will not need them, and will be worshipping with eyes closed, the words coming not just from memory but from somewhere deep within it. One scholar of charismatic spirituality suggests that the common habit of singing songs several times through is not repetition so much as accumulation and reinforcement, through which the meaning of the words is intensified and taken in more deeply.[2] The repetition of liturgy has the same effect, and even more so if it is so deeply ingrained that we know it by heart.

I think there is much value in those who lead services learning part of the text too. A pet hate of mine is being given the absolution or the blessing by someone with their nose in a book, their hands in their pockets, and their mind, by the sound of it, on the latest cricket score. I don't suppose forgiveness is affected objectively one little bit, but I certainly *feel* more forgiven when the absolution is given by someone who looks me in the eye and tells me with authority in their voice of the Lord's mercy and grace (it's an added bonus for me if they use the sign of the cross to remind me of the basis of that free forgiveness). For that reason I've learned the ASB absolution, as well as many of the blessings, Peace introductions and Eucharistic invitations, off by heart, so that I can actually say the words to people rather than read them into the air somewhere.

3. Worship with it!

We've already mentioned the fact that the whole service should be worship, but very often this just doesn't work out in practice. In a good charismatic church you can get a crude but reliable guide to what is worship and what is not by counting the number of hands in the air at any given point. If your church is anything like ours, you'll notice very quickly that worship songs *are* worship, but that notices, hymns (apart from 'Crown him with many crowns') and, above all, liturgical bits are not. When we reach the *Sanctus* in the middle of the Eucharistic prayer ('Holy, holy, holy Lord, God of power and might'), there is not an elevated digit to be seen, but if we then go on to sing a song with almost identical words everyone's away and you can't see the back wall through the forest of hands which suddenly sprouts up. OK, there's more to worship than raised hands, but why do we make it look as if we switch on for songs and off for the rest? And why does liturgy appear to be the biggest turn-off of the lot? I suspect there are two primary reasons.

The first has to do with permission. Do people know that they are allowed to worship through liturgy? If you are a leader, maybe you could give specific permission during teaching or preaching on worship, and back it up by showing some physical involvement and by saying your parts of the liturgy as if you were worshipping. This simple step could go a long way towards making the whole service seem more like worship.

The second reason, I suspect, is about instrumentation. In many churches where traditional music coexists peacefully (or otherwise) with more modern songs, the musical parts of the service are often dished out so that the organist and choir handle hymns and liturgy (if any of it is sung) while the worship group handle the 'charismatic' songs and choruses. This way of doing things indirectly tells people that they are only allowed to worship when the group is playing and not when the 'proper' musicians are at it. If we want worship to pervade the whole service, we need to explore possibilities of mixing things up a bit so that organ and group play together occasionally, the group alone handle some bits like the *Sanctus* or *Gloria,* and some of the worship songs are arranged in parts for the choir. This will confuse the congregation thoroughly, but hopefully it will lead them to the point of worshipping throughout the entire service rather than switching off completely at certain points. Although it can be difficult to get organists to do this sort of thing, it is something to aim for if you want to make the whole of your acts of worship into acts of worship.

The ultimate responsibility lies with the leaders, not just to teach people how to worship through liturgy, nor even just to show them how themselves, but also to lead the liturgy in such a way that people are inspired to join in with the worship you are already offering as you take the service.

4. Jump off it!

This section applies more to members of congregations than those up front during services – if leaders took this particular bit of advice it could get really chaotic! What I mean is that the liturgy can be used as a springboard for your own prayers and meditations. If, as you are proceeding through the service, something strikes you which you want to dwell on for a while longer, stay with it, and let the rest go on for a few minutes without you. For example, if during the introduction to the penitential section you suddenly remember an old friend from way back with whom you had an unresolved conflict, or that GBH charge which you'd quite forgotten about since you became a Christian, it may be more positive all round if you treated those thoughts not as a rather tiresome interruption to what you're supposed to be concentrating on, but as a prompting of the Spirit to prayer and even possibly action. Again, if one line or phrase from, say, the *Gloria* or a collect suddenly strikes you in a new way, stay with it and meditate for a while on the new facet of truth which has been revealed to you. Let the liturgy flow on around you while you deal with what the Lord has on his agenda for you, and catch the rest of the people up a few prayers later. It's fine to do that; a liturgical service should not be seen (or led) as if it were a route march, but rather as a ramble with plenty of time to stop and enjoy what you encounter on the way, be it a panoramic vista which suddenly opens up or a tiny flower which someone spots. It is sad that the rubrics which allow for silence to be kept several times during the course of the Communion service are so seldom heeded, but it is permissible for you to switch off for a while and create your own private silence.

5. Take it home

I don't mean the service book itself, of course; you should already have one of your own. I refer to the value of picking up insights gained during worship and staying with them during your own private or family devotions. Liturgical texts and books can help significantly with this. There is something about your own copy of a book which makes it special to you; I would want to encourage people to feel the special nature of liturgical texts too, and regard them as companions throughout the week rather than once-a-Sunday visitors.

One way of using the liturgy during the week is to make it the basis and framework for your own prayer life. Anglicans know this as 'saying the Daily Office', and many people find that the services of Morning or Evening Prayer form a helpful and comprehensive framework for them. The version of the offices produced by the Franciscan Order and published as *Celebrating Common Prayer*,[3] as well as other versions with a Celtic flavour, has proved extremely popular, and has led people into good habits of prayer and worship. Even on less ambitious levels it is possible to incorporate parts of the liturgy which you use on Sunday into the way you pray during the week. For example, the *Gloria* could be used occasionally, or possibly the confession or the Creed. In our family we have found in the past that this was an especially helpful thing to do with young children.

It is undoubtedly the case for all ages that use of the liturgy during the week enhances our appreciation of it on Sundays and vice versa. If the Lord speaks to you particularly through one of the texts during Sunday worship, it is valuable to stay with it and see if you can get more out of it by giving it time during the week. If something really hits you during the week and you have time to take it on board, you will come to the same text with a whole new appreciation next Sunday.

6. Experiment with it

This section is especially for those who are responsible for the formation and/or leading of a service. I have subdivided it into a further seven parts.

(i) Explore it

One of the controlling factors in the whole way in which modern liturgy is put together is flexibility, and yet in many churches the liturgy is about as flexible as the pews people sit in. There is so much on offer for us to explore, yet sadly familiarity and last-minute planning (or none at all) can often cause us to stick with the tried and tested. When we stay with what is familiar we miss out on a whole wealth of alternatives, each of which could add a new flavour and richness to worship.

One thing which puts people off using alternatives is that they are not always easy for the congregation (or the celebrant) to find. The compilers of the ASB were faced with a straight choice of putting alternatives side by side (as in the old Series I/II booklets) or putting them separately at the end. Both have advantages and disadvantages, and they plumped for the latter course of action which means that a straight service is easier and one which uses alternatives is more difficult (although it need not be impossible). With the advent of a whole new philosophy of liturgy enshrined in the 'Service of the Word' (a liturgical resource unique in that it is an authorised form of worship which doesn't contain a single word of text!) we have been forced to look at the whole way in which we use written words.

Three basic alternatives have become popular. The first, aided by the availability of texts on disk, is to produce a complete service sheet each week with everything on it – liturgical texts, songs, hymns and even notices. Another alternative, which is kinder to the rain forests, is to build up a set of different services for use at different times in the year. So a Communion liturgy for Lent, which might be colour-coded on mauve paper, would omit the *Gloria* and perhaps give more attention to creative ways of doing the penitential section, while another booklet, of a different colour, would be adapted for services at which all ages were present.

Home-produced service books such as these are often done on a 'bare essentials' basis: the congregation don't need to know or have in front of them every last word of the service; they simply need the bits they are to join in with, and enough of a cue to help them to do so at the right place. So for example the Eucharistic prayer, which might take two pages or more if printed out in full, could simply be presented as shown opposite.

This has the added advantage of fitting with any of the four currently authorised ASB Eucharistic prayers. Other non-congregational texts could also be omitted, although before you take this step it is worth asking some questions about the value to people of having the full text as opposed to bare essentials open in front of them. There are good arguments both ways. We in fact use a mixture of both approaches.

The third, somewhat more radical method is to abandon books altogether and put everything up on the wall on OHP slides. We do this occasionally too, and like all methods it has its strengths and weaknesses. It presupposes that your church architecture allows you to use an OHP at all (many don't), and that you have someone to operate it who is liturgically aware and alert enough to keep pace with the service and pop everything up at exactly the right time.

The Lord is here!
His Spirit is with us!
Lift up your hearts.
We lift them to the Lord.
Let us give thanks to the Lord our God.
It is right to give him thanks and praise.

The President continues the Prayer...

...for ever praising you and singing:

Holy, holy, holy Lord,
God of power and might,
Heaven and earth are full of your glory.
Hosanna in the highest.
Blessed is he who comes in the name of the Lord.
Hosanna in the highest.

The President continues the Prayer...

...Do this, as often as you drink it,
in remembrance of me.

Christ has died.
Christ is risen.
Christ will come again.

The President concludes the Prayer, with either:

...now and for ever. **Amen.**

or:

...we worship you, Father Almighty, in songs of
everlasting praise:

Blessing and honour and glory and power
be yours for ever and ever. Amen.

Reading from an OHP can be much more difficult for children: if there is a book twelve inches from their nose very little can get in between them to provide a distraction, whereas a wall forty feet away may be nothing more than a backdrop for all the other interesting things going on in the much more immediate vicinity. But if successful, the OHP method does do away with the need to handle books, announce page numbers, and so on.

Another factor to consider in the presentation of texts is what has been called the 'digital watch syndrome'. I once heard of a lecture given by a keen conservationist 'Friends of the Earth' character in which he asked the audience how many of them were wearing digital watches. As you might imagine, quite a few hands went up, which prompted the lecturer to tell their owners that they were destroying time. What he meant was that an analogue watch, while telling you the current time, does also give you a pictorial or analogical representation of what has been and what is coming. In other words the hands moving physically round the face of the watch, however slowly, do speak of the passage of time from the past, through the present to the future. Digital watches, on the other hand (on the other arm?) show you only the present moment: nothing has been, and nothing is going to be. All the watch face shows you is that right now it is 4:29. Whether or not you follow the rather convoluted logic of this argument, the fact remains (and we have already discussed it) that our post-modern world is only really interested in the here and now, with no sense of history or rootedness in the past and little interest in the approaching future. I'm not certain that this way of thinking can be directly blamed on the Casio Company, but it does provide an evocative picture of the way we treat time.

The problem with OHPs is that they treat liturgy in this way. In a book, the things you've just finished saying are still there, and if you want to you can peep ahead and look at what you're going to be saying soon. But when your liturgy is projected onto the wall, only the current, present piece of text is available. Past and future have no way of making themselves present other than through memory. You may not feel that this is a major disadvantage, but it does mean that to stay with a particular line which has spoken to you, as we've just suggested, is made very difficult, particularly, as is often the case, if the line or word which has hit you is one which you have not really noticed before, and of which you therefore have no memory. Similarly the link between what you do in church on Sunday and what you do at home during the week is weakened. So I personally am less keen on OHP liturgy, although it does have its uses for the occasional special item or in addition to text printed in the book (we project the *Gloria* as well as printing it out, in an attempt to try to give people the idea that it is a worship song!).

A word about copyright might be in order here. Official Anglican liturgical texts may be reproduced for regular use (as opposed to one-off, dated orders of service for special events) without special permission on two conditions: you may not produce more than 500 copies (more than sufficient for most churches, sadly), and they must contain the right copyright acknowledgement.[4] So the production of your own booklets or service sheets is perfectly acceptable, and relatively easy with a computer word-processing or DTP package.

It is slightly more difficult to use the text creatively, rather than simply to march through the books you already have, but I reckon it is well worth a bit of inconvenience to enrich the worship and give it greater integrity. So explore fully what is available, and use more than just a few little bits of it.

(ii) Sing it

It used to be considered the sole preserve of the Anglo-

Catholic branch of the church to use sung liturgy, but fortunately all that has changed now and many churches are experiencing the value of singing parts of the service. There are, for example, many settings of the Communion service intended for a range of instrumentation and in a range of styles and complexities. There are even some with a good charismatic pedigree. Some are available on recordings, so you can hear what the music ought to sound like before committing yourself to using it, and learn it much more painlessly once you have. It is worth a church having two or three settings in its repertoire, and it is best to use them in blocks rather than week by week. For example, a good use of two different settings would be to use a slightly more meditative one during Lent and Advent, and a celebratory one the rest of the time. But I would avoid using, say, four different ones each month on a rota. In my experience this just leaves people confused. Criteria for choosing a setting would be its simplicity and singability balanced against its having enough to it to stand repeated use over a long period.

There is a lot to be said for home-grown settings if any-one in your congregation writes music. The most successful ones use a simple melody line which is treated slightly differently in each section. If you are writing for a worship group as opposed to an organ there is much scope for orchestration, and a congregation can get much more excited about something which it knows has been composed from within the context of its own life, rather than by some Oxbridge professor. Nevertheless, most churches will have to rely on something composed by a 'proper' composer, and there are plenty of lovely ones on offer. For the record my own favourite (apart, of course, from the one I have written), is Patrick Appleford's *New English Mass*.[5] Since this setting doesn't have a Creed I would add the one from Betty Pulkingham's *King of Glory*[6] setting which I think is superb (although it does have a rather 'seventies' feel as it is written in modal style). But in the end it is all a matter of personal taste, and a church needs to find a setting or two which are acceptable. I'm currently thinking about a 'techno' setting so watch this space!

Having chosen a setting it will need to be taught. This will take at least three months, and it is better to do it gradually, beginning perhaps with the *Gloria* and then moving on to the *Sanctus* and including other parts as the people become more confident. Many churches take five minutes or so before the service starts to begin to teach what the people will then use liturgically later on in the worship. It may help to issue music copies to people, but this can be counter-productive. In my last church we had our words complete with musical notation written on OHP slides, and one terminally non-musical member of the church was heard to comment, 'I don't know why they've written all those dots and lines all over the words; it's hard enough trying to work out how it goes without all that in the way.' In the end, though, if the music is simple enough it can be easily learned and will stay in people's minds very successfully, as my children have proved. If you don't sing your liturgy, why not give it a try? And if you do, how about experimenting with singing some bits that are not usually sung? The Peace, a Confession, even the collects may be sung, with the music adding considerably to the effect of the words.

(iii) Do it

Liturgical purists will know that what we say in services is the *ritual*, while what we do is the *ceremonial*. Ceremonial is, of course, a dirty word in some church circles but, like non-conformists and their liturgy, we all have it. If the vicar walks in at the beginning of the service and out at the end; if the offering is brought forward and received; if people kneel (or sit) for prayer – all this is ceremonial, just as much as genuflection and making the sign of the cross. We all have ceremonial parts in our worship, so let's acknowledge the fact and make the best use of it.

Trevor Lloyd's excellent booklet *Ceremonial in Worship*[7] is well worth a read here. Each minister as well as each local church will have different ideas about what is appropriate or otherwise, but some guidelines might include doing what has to be done decently and in order, but not doing for the sake of ceremonial anything which does not need to be done; making sure that your ceremonial does not communicate something which you do not actually believe theologically, either in terms of doctrine or, more subtly, in terms of priesthood; and making sure that it adds to the worship of the living God rather than detracting from it and becoming an end in itself. Again, just for the record, my own personal list of babies thrown out with the 'low-church' bath water would include the sign of the cross given during the absolution and blessing and made by the people in response, processions, and kneeling for prayer. It's great that many churches are very relaxed and informal in their worship nowadays, but it would be sad if charismatic Christians forgot how to get physically on their knees before the Lord.

I could say a lot more here about the environment for worship: banners, vestments and robes, liturgical colours and so on, but I'm not really very qualified in those areas, although I know what I like. These things are important, though, and need to be thought through seriously, especially by those whose more low-church background makes them put such things fairly near the bottom in the list of priorities for the life of the church. I'll simply leave you with two comments from friends which have stayed with me and have been very important in my own pilgrimage.

The first was from a young Anglo-Catholic curate whom I met shortly after I began to become interested in the Church of England's way of doing things. He was a bit of a country bumpkin who had come up to London for his first job. Explaining why he liked liturgical colour, he said it reminded him of the seasons of the year, and the way that nature and the countryside change colour according to the season. To see the same happen in church spoke to him of the marvellous creativity of God. The other comment was from a friend who taught English and drama. She described the celebration of the Eucharist as the most incredible piece of drama ever.

Something about both these ideas grabbed me, and has deeply affected the way I feel about, and celebrate, Communion. It really upsets me when the Eucharist is handled with about as much dignity as the celebrant would use at the kitchen table making himself a bacon sandwich. Ceremonial matters; let's work at getting it right.

(iv) Select and emphasise

We touched on this when we discussed planning for worship, so I needn't say a whole lot more about it now. But briefly, I would want to argue that it can be a mistake to go straight through everything in the book on every occasion. When different themes are being emphasised in the preaching, why not emphasise them liturgically too? Why not spend some time really making something of the Creed, perhaps by singing it, or a song with similar content, or by taking it apart clause by clause and meditating on it quietly? Then you could make up for the time by simplifying the intercessions into nothing more than a minute or two for silent prayer.

Different seasons lend themselves to this policy too, as we've mentioned. During Lent and Advent you may want to take more time over the Penitential section and omit a hymn, one of the readings, or the Creed. I find it helpful to think of the balance which a liturgical framework for the service provides as being worked out not over a period of one service but during a month or two. Thus it is possible to miss out the Prayer of Humble Access for one or even a couple of weeks, as long as it isn't absent for months at a time. Taken over a longer period every part of the service is there, although not every part will be there every week.

(v) Replace it

What I mean by replacement is simply using songs which have similar sentiments to certain parts of the liturgy rather than those parts themselves. Many of us, of course, have been doing something like this for decades with material from *Psalm Praise*[8] which, as well as containing up-to-date (or at least up-to-1973) versions of many of the psalms, also has settings of the non-Eucharistic canticles. The most famous and widely used today is probably 'Tell out my soul' (the *Magnificat*), but others have caught on and are still popular.

Although our modern worship songs are not generally settings of the exact words of the liturgical texts, it is still possible to use songs which are close in vocabulary and feel. So, for example, you might replace the *Gloria* with any number of songs which praise God and celebrate his glory, or the Creed with one of the many songs which make a statement of faith. Similarly there are an increasing number of penitential songs which might be used to good effect. When we have Communion services at which our children are present (usually on the Sundays after Christmas and Easter and through August) we replace the *Sanctus*, *Benedictus* Acclamations and the bit at the end of the first Eucharistic prayer from Rite A which I've never discovered a technical name for and which we therefore call the *Terminus*, with three verses of the song:

Holy, holy, holy is the Lord
Holy is the Lord God Almighty
Who was, and is, and is to come
Holy, holy, holy is the Lord

Jesus, Jesus, Jesus is the Lord...

Glory, glory, glory to the Lord...

Used sparingly, replacement can be a very effective way of linking liturgy with modern worship. You could even go really wild by using one of these songs to replace a liturgical text and then leading into other songs in a worship slot.

We've also discussed the possibility of using replacement in spoken rather than sung texts. As liturgy moves further away from using set texts and towards the framework-and-resource-book approach of *Patterns for Worship* and the 'Service of the Word', this kind of pick'n'mix approach to liturgy will become more and more the norm. Apart from the official Anglican books,[9] CPAS's *Church Family Worship*[10] and the Franciscan *Celebrating Common Prayer*[11] are particularly helpful here, and as parts of the charismatic song-writing scene become increasingly 'liturgical', you could occasionally include parts in weekly worship. In his various 'March for Jesus' works Graham Kendrick has included some fine liturgical passages (as well as some straight pinches from the Anglican liturgy) and I see no reason why they should not be pinched back to add a new dimension to liturgical worship. It is also possible to move in another direction and find much that is helpful. One Advent we replaced our intercessions with a responsive version of the Roman Advent Antiphons,[12] and more recently we constructed the liturgy for a Maundy Thursday Agapé around the Russian Orthodox *Liturgy of St John Chrysostom and St Basil the Great*.

I wouldn't like to see replacement happening to the extent that the normal liturgy becomes redundant and people never know what they are going to get each week. A careful use of replacement, however, can be very effective now and again.

(vi) Regroup it

Later on I'll be talking about the problems of the 'hymn sandwich' approach to worship structure, but for now let me say that it is possible, and at times very effective, to use all the set parts but in a different order. This happens to some degree in Rite A with the movable Penitential section, and also in the current Initiation services, but it is in the non-sacramental services that it is most useful. The first part of Morning and Evening Prayer is a bit of an up-and-down affair with readings, canticles and a psalm coming hot foot after one another. So why not have a psalm and the readings together, as in the Eucharistic Ministry (or Liturgy) of the Word, with space for meditation in between, and then respond to the readings in worship, perhaps beginning with a canticle and launching off into a worship slot? Alternatively you could use the responses ('O Lord open our lips...') as a very appropriate lead-in to spoken and sung praise, which then moves into listening to the Bible readings. This is all fairly simple, but it seems that clergy actually need permission to feel they can do this sort of thing. It's OK, you can, and you can legally. I'll explain how shortly.

(vii) Add to it

Comprehensive though modern liturgical collections are, they often miss out totally one worship ingredient: the chance for a good long blast of celebratory praise. Liturgist Michael Vasey identifies a strand within traditional Anglican spirituality of 'a reserve that regards praise as unmanly and unnecessary – God is a well-bred Englishman'; but notes also some signs of 'a shift in liturgical style from a male military and civic liturgical style to one that is more lyric and erotic'.[13]

The New Man, apparently, no longer works totally cerebrally to avoid those terrifyingly embarrassing things

called 'feelings', so the New Anglican can now begin to
experiment with heartfelt praise. Liturgists are even writing
texts to help him!

But outside the set texts, there is still scope for learning
from the New Churches and building in a worship slot
with several songs one after the other, providing the opportunity for the congregation really to let go and celebrate,
adore or whatever. Within the overall framework, for
example of Rite A, there are several places where such a
time might be added in a way which contributes positively
to the flow of the service. How about the following?

● For five minutes before and ten minutes into the service,
  in place of the opening hymn.
● Instead of (or as well as) the *Gloria*, leading into the
  Collect and readings.
● Launching off from the Creed.
● Beginning from the Peace instead of the offertory
  hymn, and leading up to the offertory sentence, for
  example the climactic 'Yours, Lord, is the greatness...'.
● Launching off from the *Sanctus* in the middle of the
  Eucharistic prayer.
● Building slowly from the quietness of the
  administration of Communion and ending exuberantly
  with the Blessing and Dismissal.

If all this fails, you could always have a time of worship
after the service has ended!

But what about the legality of all this? While many
Anglican clergy have no conscience whatsoever about doing
anything they feel like in worship, others may regard the
suggestions I've made as outrageously illegal and therefore
quite unacceptable. There is in fact nothing in what I've
said which transgresses Canon Law, and a careful reading of
the rubrics and the *Canons of the Church of England*[14] can
help salve the consciences of the scrupulous.

First, the texts themselves often allow for the omission of many sections: in the ASB, parts with numbering in blue rather than black are optional. Along with this go the frequent rubrics allowing 'other suitable words'[15] and the very important permission given in Canon B5 to the minister to 'make and use variations which are not of substantial importance in any form of service prescribed'.[16] In extreme cases it is up to the bishop to decide whether or not the alterations are of 'substantial importance', but I doubt if he'd want to know about your using a song containing the words 'Lord, have mercy on us' instead of the Kyries (which you are allowed to omit in any case). Personally I feel that one service which I attended where they dispensed with the Eucharistic prayer and went straight to the breaking of bread had overstepped the mark, but the Canon is gloriously vague and can cover a multitude of things which are therefore not sins. The only stipulation is that any variations made 'shall be reverent and seemly and shall be neither contrary to, nor indicative of any departure from, the doctrine of the Church of England'.[17] Between them these allowances give permission to do quite a bit with the Communion service.

The Offices are slightly more difficult, but the way to cope is to obey Canon B5 again, where the minister is allowed 'on occasions for which no provision is made... [to] use forms of service considered suitable by him to those occasions'.[18] This is the Canon which allows such things as family services, sacramental confessions, and so on, and could equally well apply to a more informal 'praise service' or whatever you want to call it. And having set up your praise service, you are of course perfectly entitled to use parts of existing texts during the course of it, for example some bits of Morning or Evening Prayer.

All this may appear to be a rather questionable exercise in bending rules in order totally to break the spirit of the law, but in fact it is the very opposite – an experimentation within rules which seeks to make worship more appropriate for God's people. And it is this very exercise which the Liturgical Commission themselves are engaged in. There is a constant process of restructuring and experimentation going on, and they are aware of the widespread use of different forms of service. Rather than making people feel guilty and secretive about what they are doing, they are often glad to hear about examples of creative liturgy and about how they were received by the congregation. The liturgical books (or floppy disks) of the future are going to be much more open and flexible than the ASB, as they opt for a 'resource book' approach rather than a straightforward set of rites. The days of fossilised liturgy are over, and the creative use of words, music and action in some of the ways I've suggested, far from being frowned upon as illegal, is actually being acknowledged as pioneering for the future.

What matters supremely, however, is that those who work creatively with the liturgy do so carefully, appropriately, and with great understanding of the principles involved. One of my hobbies is Indian cookery, a cuisine based on the delicate blending of spices and flavours. An experienced chef will never use recipe books, but will work by instinct and tradition. But, as I have found to my cost, attempts to emulate the masters can either work or not. Too little spice leaves a flat, bland taste, and too much can create an overkill effect. Getting it just right takes great skill, and I fail as often as I succeed. Spicing up the liturgy is a similarly skilled process. The master chefs of the Liturgical Commission know what they are doing, and have served us up a real feast in their many publications. To try to improve on it is fine, as long as we don't spoil it in the process.

I hope you can see, then, that I am not one of those who consider it clever to play fast and loose with the law of the Church, but I do believe in using to the full the opportunities it allows me to work as skilfully as I can at making the worship of the people in my care more and more appropriate, more and more a vehicle through which they can meet God, and increasingly attractive to those as yet outside the church or the kingdom.

Notes

1 Preface to the *Alternative Service Book 1980*, p 11.
2 Barry Liesch, *People in the Presence of God* (Grand Rapids, MI: Zondervan, 1988).
3 *Celebrating Common Prayer* (London: Mowbrays, 1992).
4 The correct wording is: *The Alternative Service Book 1980* [and/or name(s) of other book(s)], material from which is included in this service, is/are copyright © The Central Board of Finance of the Church of England, 1980 [and/or other dates].
5 Patrick Appleford, *New English Mass* (London: Josef Weinberger, 1973).
6 Betty Pulkingham, *The King of Glory Setting* (Yeldall: Celebration Services, 1975). This was written for the Series 3 Communion, but is easy enough to adapt.
7 Trevor Lloyd, *Ceremonial in Worship* (Nottingham: Grove, 1981).
8 *Psalm Praise* (London: Falcon, 1973).
9 Apart from the ASB itself, other authorised or commended texts are to be found in *Lent, Holy Week and Easter: Services and Prayers* (London: Church House Publishing, 1984), *The Promise of His Glory* (London: Church House Publishing, 1990) and *Patterns for Worship* (London: Church House Publishing, 1995).
10 *Church Family Worship* (London: Hodder & Stoughton, 1986).
11 *Celebrating Common Prayer: A version of the Daily Office SSF* (London: Mowbray, 1992).
12 This text is available in David Silk, *Prayers for Use at the Alternative Services* (London: Mowbray, 1980) pp 25f and in a slightly different version in *The Promise of His Glory* pp 112ff.
13 Michael Vasey, *Worship as Communication*. Unpublished

paper from the Society for the Study of Theology, 1997.

14 *The Canons of the Church of England* (London: SPCK, 1969 but updated regularly). For a useful commentary on the Canons as they relate to worship, see Michael Perry, *A Handbook of Parish Worship* (London and Oxford: Mowbrays, 1977) pp 1–8.

15 For example ASB p 128 section 30 at the Peace. I don't believe this rubric refers solely to the alternatives provided at section 83.

16 *Canons* p 9.

17 *Ibid* p 9f.

18 *Ibid* p 9.

8

Leading Worship

1. Verbal

So you're going to lead worship. You've planned it all carefully; you have a strategy for coping with the unexpected, and now the fateful time has come for you to stand up in front of the congregation and lead them into the presence of God. How do you do it? I want to move on to attempt to answer this question, and for convenience I've split it into two different sections: this chapter will deal with specifically non-musical parts, and then the next will look more closely at music. Once again I want to attempt to be helpful to people involved in different styles of worship, so if some sections don't apply to you, feel free to give them a miss. But first, some general comments.

1. Preparation

Before you get anywhere near the service, you should have prepared for it adequately. Personal preparation is important; are you OK with the Lord, or out of touch? Have you just had a row with your wife and kids? Have you come straight from a heavy session of counselling, with someone reliving their birth experiences all over your floor? How much sleep did you get last night? All these factors and many more besides will affect not just the way in which you may 'perform' up front in a service, but also the way in which you'll plan for it in advance. Some things you'll be able to deal with, through prayer, repentance, or whatever, but others will mean that you need an even greater degree of reliance on God's grace. I find it a helpful insight, and one which I owe again to John Wimber, that we can function 'in role' as well as 'under anointing'. Sometimes you will be aware of the Spirit resting powerfully on you as you minister, but at others you will feel nothing at all, or even worse. In those instances God honours the 'role' you have in that context – that of 'service leader' – or whatever and great things can still happen.

What about those times when you feel so out of touch with God that you hardly even believe in him any more? We have all heard those we've been counselling telling us that they feel totally unable to come to church any more, since it has all become so unreal to them. Taking part in a service would feel simply like going through the motions, and would surely be nothing short of hypocritical. If such feelings make it difficult for people in the congregation, how much worse it is when the worship leader loses his faith!

If this is a long-term on-going problem, it may well be right to take some time out of ministry (for as long as you are able), and to seek help from someone you trust. But for those times when our depression is simply a phase through which we are passing, there is real merit in keeping going and putting on a brave face. I can remember clearly one day (it was a Tuesday) waking up in the morning to find I didn't believe in God. I just turned over, opened my eyes, yawned, and became an atheist. Unfortunately, it was a really bad time to stop believing in God, because I had five outside speaking engagements that week. That evening I had to go to Swanwick conference centre with our worship team to lead the clergy at a diocesan conference in worship, the next night I had to give an evangelistic talk on 'The God of

Miracles', I had a day on the healing ministry, and a couple of others I can't now remember. What on earth could I do? I couldn't pray about it, since atheists don't believe it'll make any difference; I really thought it would be unkind to ring up five organisers and say 'I'm supposed to be coming to you but I'm afraid I've stopped believing in God' – that would really drop them in it. In the end, through nothing whatsoever but sheer cowardice, I decided that I was enough of a professional to go through the motions. The God I didn't believe in would understand, surely. So I stood up in front of the clergy with my guitar and invited them to exalt the Lord and worship his holy name; I preached on the God who still worked miraculously today, and so on. Believe me, playing the guitar with your fingers crossed behind your back is not an easy thing to do!

That week was one of the most powerful I can remember in my entire ministry. There was such a mighty moving of the Spirit at each of the meetings. Night after night we prayed and ministered to people, and saw all sorts of people receive a touch from his hand. We saw healings, deliverances, people finding God. It was just like the book of Acts all over again. By the end of the week I had seen so much of God at work that I believed in him again, and have continued to do so ever since!

So if you feel you are losing your faith, keep going. First the discipline is very helpful at such times, and can stop a dangerous and insidious process of drifting out of church attendance. Secondly it can often be the case that our own 'hypocritical' worship leading can be the very thing which lifts our spirit up to God again. As we're exhorting and encouraging the congregation to worship, we may suddenly find that we've talked ourselves into it too! I find it more positive at such times to think not in terms of hypocrisy, but rather of offering a sacrifice of praise to the Lord. It was John Wesley who said, 'Preach faith until you have it.' The same principle applies to worship leading. And thirdly, when all is said and done, if every minister who was feeling out of touch with God were to stop functioning until they felt better, the whole of Christendom would collapse within about three weeks. The Enemy knows how fragile we are emotionally, especially when we're about to go out on public view. That's why he always makes our spouses or friends function at their most abrasive just as we're leaving home for the service. Many worship leaders begin to praise the Lord with the sound of angry words and a slammed front door still ringing in their ears. If we give in too easily to the Enemy, he's got us just where he wants us. So deal with what you can; what you can't deal with, forget for now and get on with the job in hand, which is to glorify God.

Another part of preparation is planning the service. We've already discussed this in some detail so I won't say any more now. But it should go without saying that a service very often tends to run better if we've not only chosen the hymns, readings and so on beforehand, but also communicated that fact to the organist, readers and other interested parties.

Finally, and this is the most neglected part of the preparation, you need to do the last minute getting together of everything you're going to need. All the necessary books should be ready, with markers in the places you're going to need to find. The hymn book should be open to the first hymn you're going to use, and the scraps of paper people have handed you with notices on should be neatly clipped together. Other people taking part should be aware that you're expecting them, and when. All this is obvious, but we still don't do it. We nip back into the vestry during hymns to get things we've forgotten; we have times of silence not so much that the Spirit can move, but so that we can find the right page; we forget to read the banns of marriage. All of this can be avoided if we take time before the service to prepare. One Anglican clergyman, about to commence a baptism, suddenly realised with horror that he'd forgotten to fill the font. Pondering momentarily on a theology of dry-cleaning rather than washing, he decided that the only way to redeem the situation was through sheer bluff, so he ordered the congregation, 'Please stand for the ceremony of the fetching of the water!' and processed in a dignified manner to the tap. I doubt whether anyone even noticed, but such situations are not really ideal. I find it helpful to think through each part of the service, checking that I've got everything I'm going to need.

2. First impressions

I've mentioned already my difficulty in defining 'presence', but I do know some things I can do to help, and I need to make sure I do them very quickly as the service begins. As an Anglican priest I have responsibility for anything up to seventy weddings each year, and I'm aware that as I stand up at the start of each one I'm faced with a church full of people with all sorts of things going on in their heads. The vast majority of them are not Christians; they may be feeling horribly out of place in church; they will have expectations about how the service will feel, what a vicar will be like, how long they have to put up with this before they can get back to the beer, and so on. I'm also aware that their impressions will be confirmed or shattered within a very short time of the start of the service, perhaps even a matter of seconds rather than minutes. So I go all out to be the best I can be right from square one. I look round, I smile at them, I open my mouth to speak, and I make sure they can hear right from the very first word. Drawing myself up to my full height, I boom out with the butchest and most unparsonical voice I can manage, 'Welcome to St James'….' I'm wanting to relax people by letting them know they're in my hands, and that I can handle it. Whenever people tell me later what a 'nice service' it has been, I believe I convinced them of that literally within the first thirty seconds of it. By contrast, a weedy, uncertain, inaudible start can lose people in a way which makes them next to impossible to recapture. What is true for outsiders at weddings is to a lesser extent true for attenders at all services. Presence is nowhere more essential than at the very start.

It's worth saying something briefly at this stage about microphone technique, since many churches nowadays do use PA, or at least attempt to use it. By far the best system for the service leader is to use a radio microphone. This means that you are totally free of wires, and can wander about at leisure with no drop in sound volume, but it does have several drawbacks. Radio mikes are notoriously unreliable, and can fizz and crackle throughout the service, especially if you have something metal too near the transmitter. Anything from chair legs to loose change can make the service sound as if it is being broadcast live from Beijing or somewhere. And of course they can be very expensive. The PA operator needs to be on the ball, since the only time it is absolutely guaranteed to work is before the service starts, and it can be most unedifying if the waiting congregation pick up at full volume everything from the prayer in the vestry that God will give the so-and-sos a good shaking tonight, to the pre-service trip to the loo. The next best thing is a trailing halter mike, which is considerably cheaper but does limit mobility. The ceremonial unplugging at the chancel step and replugging at the altar can add something to the liturgy (usually two loud thumps), but once again an operator who is on the ball can close the mike during the process. If you use ordinary stand mikes, you need to make sure that you are the right distance and direction from them when you speak. Different mikes vary, and you will need to get to know yours, but on average your mouth should be about six to eight inches away from and three to four inches above the end of the mike. If you are too close the congregation will hear your heavy breathing, and if you are not far enough above the mike, there will be a clap of thunder every time you use a word with a 'p' in it. Some mikes have a built-in 'pop-shield' to prevent this; if not, you can get external ones – little sponge rubber hats which fit over the business end. You can even get them in the correct liturgical colours. Having positioned yourself correctly, the art is simply to forget that the mike is there, and speak as normally as you can. It is not enough just for you to be able to use mikes correctly; you also need to train and practise with anyone who will speak into one during the service. Lesson readers and intercessors can be notoriously bad at it.

Good PA is very important, since it is an unchangeable law of the church that those with the most severe hearing difficulties always sit nearest the back. The sound level should be comfortable for everyone. If you do have an elderly congregation it may be worth considering an induction loop system in all or a part of your building. This is basically a loop of wire under the floor or around the walls which gives a signal which many hearing aids can pick up. Specialist firms will be glad to advise you about a system like this. But whatever you use, it should be as unobtrusive as possible, so that it adds to rather than detracts from the sense of worship.

3. Body language

The general rubrics to the Anglican ASB Rite 'A' Communion Service specify that '...the president may use traditional manual acts during the Eucharistic Prayers'. I've said a bit about this in the previous chapter, but it is worth making the point that a good worship leader will be involved physically as well as verbally in the service. Whether or not you go in for the works in terms of ceremonial, it is important that what you are saying with

your body backs up and illustrates what you are saying
with your mouth. Many people lead worship figuratively (if
not literally) with their hands in their pockets, and this
cannot help but communicate to the congregation that they
are not really interested in what they are doing. In whatever
way is appropriate in your setting for you to do it, you
need to communicate involvement, excitement and participation in worship. In this way you will give a good lead to
the congregation to become fully involved. This applies not
just during Eucharistic Prayers, but throughout everything
you do.

4. A service, not a meeting

There is all the difference in the world between 'taking a
service' and 'leading worship'. The former implies that
there are certain things to be got through during the next
hour, rather like items on an agenda, whereas the latter
implies that everything we do and say should be centred
around the theme of the service and aimed at leading people
into the presence of God so that he can be lifted up among
us. It is a rare skill to be able to make everything, notices
and banns included, into part of an act of worship, but it
can be done, and it should be our aim to do it. The way in
which we conduct things, including ourselves, should point
to God and should express some truth about him which
people, whether they know him or not, should be able to
take on board. So how might we do it?

The welcome and introduction should be welcoming and
introductory, since they are the first things people will hear
you say. I have taken many services where the very first
thing people have heard me say (or rather sing) was 'O
Lord, open thou our lips...' Let's just stop for a moment
and listen to what I was actually saying...

Well, here we all are again. We're starting on page 19, but

there's no need to tell you that, because you all know it. You're the same people who were here last week when we started on page 19, and in fact every week since 1662 when the words were first said. You know you're welcome, so there's no need to spell it out, although it would have saved us all a lot of bother if you hadn't come. Never mind, here you are, so we'd better get on with it. If by any unimaginable chance you are new here and don't know what on earth is going on, tough. You'll just have to *feel* welcome, and try to peer over to the nearest person five pews away to find out what page we're starting on, or even which book we're in. 'And our mouth shall shew forth thy praise...'

Hardly welcoming or introductory, is it? This whole approach works on the assumption that no one will ever be present at a service who is not a regular attender. Very often it is a true assumption, and it is easy to see why. So let's take the trouble to welcome people if they really are welcome, and to give them at least a vague clue as to what they might expect to happen and how they might join in if they feel like it. Sometimes it is a good idea to begin with what Anglicans call 'the Peace', and to give people a chance to greet one another. This establishes a corporate feel to the service right from the start, and in my experience lifts considerably any singing which is to follow.

There seems to be two equal and opposite errors in the announcing of hymns. The first is simply to say, 'Hymn number 239,' and the second is to preach a sermon about the theology of the hymn, the biography of its author, the musical merits of the tune, and how you like it because you had it at your wedding. Probably there is a middle way which gives some idea as to why you have chosen this particular hymn, and how it reflects the theme of the service, but which doesn't make the actual singing of it seem like a bit of an anticlimax when you finally get round to it. Your introduction should help people to experience singing the hymn as a part of their worship, as they realise how it moves them further along and deeper into the unfolding theme of the service. It also helps if instructions about posture are given as the last thing you say before they start, and not the first. If you say 'Let's stand to sing "Great is thy faithfulness", and then go on to say a bit about it, you leave people hovering somewhere between sitting and standing, which is not only embarrassing for them, but also very bad for the back. So say what you want to say, and then round it off with 'So let's stand to sing....' That way everyone knows where they are.

When it comes to prayers and bits of liturgy there are a variety of different ways of getting people to begin speaking at the same time. The most widely practised is for the leader to begin with the first line, speaking in a slightly slower and more emphatic tone of voice, so that people can join in with the second phrase:

Leader: Almighty God,
All: to whom all hearts are open...

But there are other ways of doing it. You can announce the fact that you are going to use the Collect for Purity, and then give a cue for people to begin:

Leader: Together ...
All: Almighty God, to whom all hearts are open...

The disadvantage of this model is that it sprinkles the liturgy with several 'Togethers' which, after a while, take on an almost liturgical feel themselves. The other main way of doing it is for the leader to say the first line, which the congregation repeat after him:

Leader: Almighty God,
All: Almighty God, to whom all hearts are open...

This works fine as long as everyone knows the rules, but if you have in your midst anyone who is used to the first and by far most common model, you set up a wonderful fugal effect as he carries on from line two while everyone else goes back and repeats line one. In the end, the majority tends to win, but it can be rather unseemly for a few seconds while the competition is going on. All in all I prefer the first way, which, although it has the disadvantage that the people never get to say 'Almighty God', seems to me to outweigh the other models, not least because it is the most widely practised. It is important, though, to be consistent, so that, as it were, everyone knows the rules. Once the prayer gets going, the leader needs to make sure that he leads clearly, and avoids idiosyncratic pace or phrasing, but rather sets the speed and follows the natural rhythm and pauses of the words. Clergy seem to be notoriously bad at this, and they get worse as they get older. Not only should the leader be leading the people, he should also be listening to them, and listening especially for any tendency to leave them behind or drag behind them.

When everyone is joining together in a piece of liturgy, it is good to encourage them from time to time to say it as if they mean it. Years ago I experienced a 'performance' of one of the *Make Way!* marches which affected profoundly the way in which I lead liturgy. It contains several 'liturgical' passages, some of them lifted straight from Anglicanism, but rather than being used as bits to say together, they are used as triumphant shouts or as heartfelt prayers. It made me realise how unconvincing much of our liturgy must sound to God, and the following Sunday I led the congregation at my church in 'shouting' Psalm 96 together. This was obviously new to most, but I could see from people's faces how much they were enjoying it. I certainly found a new depth of meaning in the words as they were spoken with the gusto which they deserve.

Congregational praying is something which can also be

handled in different ways. How can you pray together as a church in a way which feels together, but which also allows for maximum participation? There is a fundamental tension here, and it is one which increases with the size of the congregation. Do you have someone 'up front' articulating the prayers of the whole congregation; would open prayer either in the whole congregation or in small groups be the best model; or should we all shout our prayers out loud at the same time as they do in Korea? I have used a variety of models, each of which has its strengths and weaknesses. We need to watch more than anything else the user-friendliness of the different models: what are your visiting banns couple going to do if asked to turn round in groups of five and pray for Zimbabwe? And is that better or worse than being asked to pray out loud at the same time as everyone else? If we are going to go for some of the more outrageous models, we probably need to provide some kind of a get-out clause and allow people to 'sit and pray quietly on your own'.

The way in which we handle the spoken parts of the service is vital if it is to lead people deeper into an awareness of God. I want to end this section by quoting a passage from a Roman Catholic book on worship, which sums up beautifully much of what I have been trying to say. If you haven't understood so far, I hope this will help:

God is dead!

God is dead... when the priest, praying to God, looks at the congregation as if to persuade them that he is.

God is dead... when soloists, or the choir, sing words to God and make music without being involved in what they are singing.

God is dead... when the reader reads from the Bible as if it were a telephone directory, without pausing for breath and without allowing the Spirit to breathe.

God is dead... when the assembly recites the Lord's Prayer or sings a hymn as if it were a popular song.

God is dead... when hymns no longer know how to speak to God and only aim to question a new moralism.

God is dead... when the priest raises his arms to shoulder height in a mechanical gesture, no longer towards a symbolic otherness, or holds out his hands over the offerings in a mechanical gesture, and not under the weight of the Spirit.

God is dead... when people speak of God, carp at God, always refer to him as 'he' and not as 'you'.

God is dead... when the word of God is not in the words, the ineffability of God is not in the silences, the Spirit is not in the bodies.

No, God is not dead, but appearances – and liturgy is all about appearances – are sometimes able to make us doubt his presence.[1]

Note

1   Jean Lebon, *Understanding the Liturgy* (London: SCM, 1987) p 58.

9

Leading Worship

2. Musical

We've talked about the liturgical and verbal parts of the service, and how to help them feel more like worship; now we turn to the more specifically musical parts. We hope, of course, that the whole service will be 'worship', but for many people music is at the heart of their response to God. I don't want to get into any arguments about terminology, so you will need to put up with me using the word 'worship' in two distinct ways: to describe the service or meeting as a whole, but also that part of it commonly designated a 'time of worship', or a 'worship slot'. In concentrating now on music, I'm not meaning to imply that anything else that happens is less glorifying to God (although it may well be in practice).

The idea of being in any way involved in leading music will, of course, give many ministers or service leaders a sense of foreboding horror, as they exclaim 'But I'm not musical!' While this may in many cases be true, it need not actually matter too much if there is someone around who is musical and who knows how to lead in such a way that the unmusical service leader can trust them. You can simply hand the leadership over for the duration of the worship slot and take it back again at the end. It is also worth investing a lot of time in your musician, since he or she will

be a very important right-hand person to you, and you will
need to build up a really empathic relationship with them.
Get them to try and drum some kind of musical 'feel' into
you, while you teach them some of the rudiments of
leadership which we discussed in the last chapter. You
should both benefit from the relationship in the long run,
although it may take years rather than months. It needs to
be said also, of course, that even if you are musical there
may still be someone else better equipped to lead the
worship slot than you, and you may need to relinquish
some of your responsibility to them from time to time.

What then is a 'worship slot', and how can you run one?
Perhaps it would be helpful to look at some different ways
in which this is done in different settings, in order both to
identify what it is we're talking about, and to look at
different 'models' which, no doubt, will all have strengths
and weaknesses. I have identified seven different models for
a worship time.

1. The 'hymn sandwich' model

This is not really a model for a worship slot as such; rather
it is its very antithesis. Both liturgical and non-liturgical
churches can fall into this trap in different ways. Basically it
is the use of music as a set of bridges to get from one item
in the service to another. It could, of course, be seen the
other way round, that the sermon, readings, notices and so
on are the bridges to get from one hymn to the other, but
either way it gets you nowhere, since you are not doing
anything in the service for long enough at a time. We've
already mentioned the Baptist church in which I was
brought up, although more deliberately liturgical services
can be just as bad. I was once involved (as I've mentioned)
in starting a new evening service in the parish church,
which was to be 'charismatic' in nature. I am basically a
liturgical creature, so I was adamant that we had to use the

framework of the Anglican Evening Prayer service. It wasn't very many weeks before we discovered the same thing as our Baptist friends, that music broken up into little bits tends to produce worship broken up into little bits, moving and wonderful though the *Magnificat* and the *Nunc Dimittis* may be. So we held onto the framework, but put all the music together and then had the readings, canticles, and so on. It made a tremendous difference to the whole service doing it that way round.

The problem is that if we want to get to the point of an encounter with God, we have to pedal very fast indeed to get there in the space of one hymn or song. Yes, the readings are still worship, but unless we are very tuned in to God, we are bound to experience a slight dropping off in the intensity of our devotion when we move from the last chorus of that latest worship song into Leviticus 13:47-59, or whatever the first reading happens to be. We're only human, and it takes time to get in touch with Almighty God, especially if we really do want intimacy with him in worship. This model allows no time, and it is best adapted for renewed worship.

2. The 'community singalong' model

Here the mistakes of the 'hymn sandwich' model have been rectified, and plenty of time is allowed for a good sing. Under the direction of an enthusiastic song leader, who is determined that everyone *will* have a good sing, the congregation goes through one piece after another, while the leader tests his ingenuity, and at the same time seeks to prevent boredom, by thinking up as many different interesting ways of singing as he can. Meanwhile, either because he thinks they need it, or because he is cold or has circulation trouble, he conducts the congregation vigorously. Arms flailing like a frenetic windmill, he encourages the singers on: 'Now the ladies only for verse eight!', 'The men this time, very quietly...', 'The chorus again, this side of the aisle...', 'Right, this side, let's see if we can do better than that...', 'The next song – only people called Arthur or Geraldine...' and so it goes on. Great fun this may be, especially for the leader, but it has one major problem: it has very little to do with worship. Whatever words the people may be singing, it is very difficult for them to take on much worship content while the singers are watching a gymnastic display, listening to a shouting contest, and trying to guess whether or not they are likely to be allowed to join in next time round. The best hope for a worshipper caught in such a session is not to be called Arthur or Geraldine and to sit the whole thing out completely, practising their Ignatian contemplative prayer exercises while the singing goes on around them. This is, of course, a caricature, but there is truth in it. It is only too easy for worship leaders to get in the way and prevent people meeting with God, however well-intentioned they may be. I will want to say in a while that there is also danger in a leadership style which has too little rather than too much visibility and verbal encouragement, but personally I would rather err on that side.

3. The 'Chinese takeaway' model

This one used to be the very favourite of informal small groups, college CUs and house fellowships. There are two variations of it. In the most pure version, the leader simply says, 'Er, has anyone got a song they'd like to sing?' After an embarrassed silence, broken only by the frantic rustling of songbook pages, someone says, 'Could we sing number 17?' More rustling as everyone else finds number 17, then off they all go. At the end of the song there is a bit more silence and rustling, then, 'Number 127?', which they dutifully sing. By now the group has got over its self-consciousness, and the real ordering begins, as people all over the room remember what number their favourite is and shout it out: '28!', '354!', '182!', they go, with great fervour. Then, the group's equivalent of the village idiot, who *always* picks number 469 every week without fail, gets to place his order, amid polite but scarcely disguised groans. So the meeting goes on until the leader thinks that everyone has had enough. He is probably right.

The second variation, for the more liberal rather than for the purists, tries to inject a little objectivity and direction into the proceedings. Obviously some prayer and planning has gone in here, as the leader confidently announces, 'I thought we'd begin with number 511.' At the end of 511 he leads smoothly into his next choice, number 217, and thence into 86. The inexperienced worshipper may at this stage begin to feel that he has accidentally stumbled upon a proper worship time, which has direction and is actually going somewhere. However, his fears are soon allayed as the leader, just as the group is beginning to get in touch with God, asks the fateful question 'Has anyone got a song they'd like to sing?' For details of the rest of the meeting, see variation (1) above.

What's the problem? This model ought to work, yet it seldom does. Surely if everyone is choosing songs which are important to them, there must be at least one person having a good time at any given moment. The difficulty lies, it seems to me, in the flow of the songs. Just because number 392 is my favourite, that doesn't mean that it has any connection in feel, theology or musical key with number 142, which was the last person's favourite, or number 5 which is going to be the next person's. If the leader goes for the second variation, it's almost worse, since you can begin to get somewhere and then be disappointed. With the first, at least you can be sure from the start that you're in for a flop.

4. The 'spontaneous' model

This model enshrines the belief that all planning is sinful, worldly, faithless and restricting for the Spirit. Failing to notice that they have a pretty restricting view of the Spirit if they think he can be restricted by their plans, *aficionados* of this model turn up to worship with nothing but an open mind, and wait for the leading of the Lord. This seems at first sight like a very biblical model; the expectation is that everyone will come along with a contribution of some sort, and that all the different contributions will flow together into a pleasing whole. And, it must be said, this does sometimes happen. The problem is, though, that it doesn't happen very often. What in fact tends to happen is that you get a variation on the 'takeaway' model, or nothing at all of any lasting devotional use. If indulged in frequently enough, the spontaneity takes on a remarkably predictable, even 'liturgical' feel, with the same songs, verses, prayers and so on coming out week after week. I am a firm believer in careful planning, because I think that in the end it allows more actual spontaneity to take place. And, I believe, it is by far the most biblical way of going about things. The 'spontaneous' model is built on one verse from 1 Corinthians 14; planning and preparation seems to me to be the hallmark of vast sections of the Old Testament, as we've already mentioned.

5. The 'Vineyard' model

When I first attended a conference run by John Wimber of the Vineyard back in 1984, and experienced their worship, I soon became aware that not only was I in for a completely new collection of songs, but also a completely new way of worshipping. Since John's first major public exposure to English Christians in late 1984, his style of music, and many of the Vineyard songs, have become extremely popular in our churches. He has a carefully thought-out theology of worship, he knows exactly what he expects to happen and how to help people to let it happen. And for thousands of people, it has happened. One friend told me, 'Vineyard worship took me to a place I've never ever been to with the Lord before.' What is this marvellous way of worshipping? Is it really as brilliant as all that?

There seems to be two keynotes: simplicity and intimacy. The aim of worship is to bless God, to let him enjoy and find pleasure in our praises; to reach the point of intimacy with him, and to have him come among the worshippers and meet with them in power. To do that, you have to strip away everything extraneous which could be a distraction from that goal of intimacy. You simply sing to the Lord, and move gradually deeper and deeper into his presence. The songs are simple, repetitive and full of emotion, and much use is made of men's and women's voices singing in canon, with the accompanying climactic points when both join in together. The worship leader's job is simply to murmur 'Number 7' before the next song (not always 'Number 7', of course; it's not that simple!). Apart from that there are no verbal interjections. (I discovered on a subsequent visit to America that even 'Number 7' is a concession for the benefit of British audiences; over there the songs are not announced at all.) The music rolls along with no perceptible direction, not even the shortest of breaks, and no sense of an approaching climax, for anything up to forty-five minutes, then it stops.

Clearly this model is a contender for a successful worship time. The exact antithesis of the 'community singalong' model, it allows the worshipper space and time with the Lord, and provides music which cannot, by its complexity, get in the way, but which is intended to carry the singer along in its flow as smoothly as possible. For many people this model has provided a way to God which is both real and exciting; for that I praise the Lord. But, dare I say it, I don't personally believe that the Vineyard has got it one hundred per cent right. I have written elsewhere a more thorough critique.[1] Without wishing in any way to detract from what has become a very important strand in British worship, I do want briefly to make some negative comments about it. I believe that there are problems to do with style of music, understanding of worship, and expectations of the worshippers.

The problem with the music (or the strength of it, depending on your point of view) is that it is all very similar. If cathedral choirs are 'Radio 3' worship, and some modern British material is 'Radio 1', Vineyard songs are definitely 'Radio 2'. As I say, this may be good or bad for you personally, depending on whether you like Terry Wogan or not, but there is nowhere near the range of feel, colour, tempo and so on of a selection of our songs. The lyrics, too, may seem simple and intimate to one worshipper, but may equally seem slushy and theologically bereft to another, especially if you have been singing them for forty-five minutes. This limiting of musical style is tied in, I think, to a limited understanding of the purposes of worship. To go back to our six categories, Vineyard music is very good on 'adoration and love'; the stream of worship flowing out from Toronto Airport ex-Vineyard has increased the number of 'celebration and joy' songs from the previous two, but that's about it. Particularly noticeable by its absence is any hint of the victorious feel of many of our warfare songs, and personally I feel that this is a serious lack.

But for me the most serious problem lies in the expectations that this model seems to have of the worshippers' spiritual stamina. The very thing which is designed to leave space for them to meet with God can in fact be that which leaves them to their own devices. No doubt you get better at it with practice, but I find it very hard to concentrate in worship for over half an hour at a time, especially when the music is so unvaried, and the direction so unspecified. I think that congregations need more help than the Vineyard would give them. But, let me say again, this is only my personal opinion; if you really love this style, praise the Lord! If you feel it could be right for your set-up, go for it. It's better than a 'Chinese takeaway', anyway.

6. The 'Spring Harvest' model

I'm slightly embarrassed by this name, but I don't really know what else to call it. I'm sure Spring Harvest isn't the only place they do it, but for me this tremendous Easter-time conference-cum-festival epitomises a way of worshipping which, while not being perfect, is the next best thing. Those who are Spring Harvest veterans will know exactly what the worship is like; for those who are not, I'll attempt to pick out some of the distinctive qualities. The father-figure is of course Graham Kendrick, although other, younger worship leaders use essentially the same model. It's not perfect, but I do feel that it combines the very best of lots of other strands, and provides the most helpful model for many of our needs today in the church.

There is, first, an extremely wide range of songs and musical styles. Traditional hymns sit comfortably alongside the most rowdy of modern choruses, and pieces with great theological stature walk hand in hand even with – yes! – Vineyard songs. Graham's partnership with black keyboard player Steve Thompson has brought some fascinating new styles into the repertoire, and with other musicians of equally high calibre the musical virtuosity can be quite stunning. This virtuosity is encouraged, and instrumental breaks lift the worship even when no words are being sung, although sensitivity is the name of the game, and the musicians are never intrusive.

Secondly, there is a clear worship leader, whose job is not just to announce the next song, nor yet to whip up human enthusiasm, but rather to encourage the worshippers by his words, to suggest new direction for their meditation or praise, to use the words and music to greatest effect, to highlight and articulate what he feels God is especially doing at the moment and, above all, to guide and lead the worship time, under the direction of the Spirit, in the way and towards the end which God has for it. The music, as in the Vineyard, is 'seamless', but this is achieved not by non-stop singing, but by skilful and sympathetic instrumentalists 'laying down a carpet' of extempore music while the leader speaks, prays, prophesies, or just asks for stillness in the congregation. One song flows neatly into the next with no awkward pauses, and the direction is maintained. Should the leader feel that the Spirit is taking them off in a new and unexpected direction, there is built-in flexibility to allow for this, but it is always flexibility with a framework, rather than the complete spontaneity which so often leads nowhere at all.

If this model has dangers, they lie in two different areas. First, the temptation, which the leader must resist at all cost, to preach a twenty-minute sermon before each song, and secondly the almost total lack of complete silence, which in fact ought to be there in our worship from time to time. But these are not intrinsic dangers in the model, they arise simply from bad use of the model, and needn't be too much of a problem for the well-trained and experienced leader.

One variation from 'pure' Spring Harvest praxis which we use at our church, and which we can use because we don't yet have 5,000 in the congregation, is what we refer to as the 'PSH'. This stands, rather irreverently some feel, for a 'Planned Spontaneous Happening'; in other words an opportunity in the middle of a worship slot for us to open up for contributions from the floor, as people are invited to express their worship in prayers or songs, or to bring a prophetic word or picture. We will deliberately build in a PSH at a climactic point in the worship, and we use it either to continue and reinforce the same direction, or alternatively to change direction. So for example, in between two adoration songs, it might be appropriate for people to express their love for the Lord out loud, as an encouragement to others. When after a few minutes the prayers stop flowing, the worship leader would either announce, or, better, simply lead into the next song, so that the flow continues. If the musicians can manage it, they could be improvising quietly under the congregation's contributions, and following the mood of what is being expressed (some of the skills of the old 'silent movie' pianist come in very handy here). Alternatively, the PSH can be a useful way of changing direction slightly. I'll say a bit more about handling contributions from the floor in a while, but I do believe it's worth the risk which can be involved in allowing space for them. Not least, it helps people not to feel that the whole thing is so sewn up that there is nothing for them to do other than accompany the musicians.

7. The 'Rave' model

One final strand has come recently with the emergence of a specific youth worship culture, based to some extent on the dance and rave scenes. Electronic technology has brought the kinds of sounds associated with these styles within easy reach of churches that are interested in reaching it, and while not being an expert, it seems to me that the whole point is to get worn out enjoying God. Bands like the Worldwide Message Tribe have an enormous following among the few teenagers left in our churches, and their music also seems to be enjoyed by people like me who are no longer quite in the 'teenage' category but really rather wish we were. Musically it is loud, fast, vibrant, and best in the dark. But it does seem to have engendered a deep spirituality in youngsters, with its major themes of total and complete commitment to God and fervent hope and prayer for revival.

Personally I love it, although it does scare me a bit. During Lent this year we had our usual austere diet of serious music on CD, deliberately chosen so that the Easter Sunday celebrations would seem so much better by comparison. At about 9.20 am on Easter Day, just ten minutes before the service was due to start, the worship leader came up to me and asked if I'd mind if they did one of the songs 'techno' style. My immediate reaction was to say no: it would be risky in our radical evening service, but at 9.30 in the morning it would finish off my career altogether. My refusal was taken in good grace, but soon afterwards I saw a horrific vision of myself as an old fogey, frightened of change, not stepping out on a limb in case it upset other people, and so on. I raced after the worship leader and told her I was sorry and that they should go for it after all. They did! It seemed to go well, and as I had a holiday straight after I could keep my head down for a while, but it was scary. The thought of holding back a church which wanted to go forward faster than I could cope with made me feel for a few moments just like an Anglican vicar!

However, to return to the 'Spring Harvest' model, I hope that I have given a fair picture of what I mean, and I hope as well that some people have recognised it and are thinking, 'But that's what we do!' It's what I do most of the time too, and it's for this model that this book is intended to provide something of a manual for leaders. This type of worship is the most demanding to lead, apart perhaps from the sheer amount of physical energy needed by the singalong leader, and therefore requires the highest degree of Spirit-led planning, and also of competence in potential leaders. We'll move on now to explore different aspects of the skills needed in order for musical worship to be led efficiently.

How might you actually lead a worship slot which looks

like this? The first question to ask is 'Who is leading it?'
Perhaps the most common scenario would be that of the
service leader working with a group of musicians and
singers which might contain the *group leader* or *musical
director* and a *worship leader* or *fronter*. Obviously there's
one vital question to sort out right from the start: who's in
charge? With so many leaders, you need to know clearly for
any worship slot who is to be given responsibility. If this is
not clearly decided, and that decision communicated to all
concerned, two opposite and equally unseemly disasters can
occur. The first is that no one leads. Awkward gaps and
silences ensue – silences quite unlike those awesome times
when the Lord is manifestly present and no one wants to
do anything except stand and enjoy him. Non-verbal
gestures of the 'After you', 'No, after you' type fly
backwards and forwards across the dais. Facial expressions
lose their spaced-out worshipping glow and become
anxious, angry and resigned by turns, and the poor congregation leave their enraptured state and open their eyes to
see what looks like a game of charades going on up front.

The other alternative is that everyone leads, and the
worship takes on a form which combines highlights of both
Wimbledon and the House of Commons, with directions,
encouragements, song announcements and so forth
bouncing around the front of the church and leaving the
congregation as a crowd of spectators with terminal neck
ache. So appoint one leader, and make sure that everyone
knows who it is. Rather than cramping people's style, this
actually encourages participation, since there is a safe and
secure framework into which to add contributions.

If the worship is to be led from within the group of
musicians, the service leader's role is easy. He simply has to
hand over to the fronter, and know when to take leadership
back again. But if the service leader is also the fronter, a
whole new problem rears its head – communication. How
can the leader direct music if he is neither a singer nor a

musician? It is not simply a case of his being able to thump out another chorus on the piano; he has to decide what he wants to do, and then let someone else know in time for them to do it. And while in some of the more meditative choruses he may have time to wander over and place his order with the musicians, generally the whole process will have to be much more speedy.

The answer in my experience is twofold. The first part is to make sure you know your starting point for each song. I don't mean by this the note you come in on (although that does add a certain something if you can get it right), but rather the basic format you'll use. On my word-processor you can set up for each document the details you want in terms of paper size, margin widths, print size, tabs and so on. But if you start a document without specifying any of these, the computer automatically puts in details it has chosen for you. This is called its 'default mode', and I find this a helpful concept for worship songs too. When we first learn a new song, we make sure that we all agree and learn its 'default mode', in other words the way we will do it in the absence of any further indication from the leader. The default mode will contain several elements: the intro, 'turnarounds' which enable you to move smoothly from both a chorus to a verse and from a chorus to another chorus, the order in which you'll do the song (verse 1, chorus, verse 2, chorus, chorus) or whatever, and the ending. It may also involve a key change halfway through or a tempo change such as slowing down the final chorus. Each song has its default mode, so if the worship leader asks for something and then gets slain in the Spirit everyone will know what to do at least until the end of the song.

But what next? That's all very well, and it does provide a good basis from which to work, but how do you communicate change as you go along, allowing for flexibility and response to what God is doing at any given moment? The second part of the answer is a set of hand

signals. Since they are done silently they don't disturb even
the quietest of songs; conversely they can make themselves
understood during even the most rousing singing, clapping
and dancing. When you get really good you can even signal
with your eyes shut, thus not interrupting your own flow
of worship, although you do need faith to believe that the
musicians have interrupted their own sufficiently to have
seen the signal. It needn't be as bad as it initially may seem;
you simply need ways of communicating basic information,
and while it might be useful to have a universal sign
language which worship groups across the globe could
understand, a kind of manual Esperanto, it's probably best
to develop your own within the church. You only need a
dozen or so signs, just so that you can say, for example, 'go
round again', 'a bit faster', 'modulate up a tone', 'play
through a verse quietly so that I can do a voice-over',
'repeat verse two', 'stop', 'unaccompanied', and so on.

We also have a very useful mouth- rather than hand-
signal which we call the 'goldfish': an exaggerated open-
mouthed gulp of air to show people at what point to begin
singing. We use the old dance-band technique of using
fingers to indicate key changes: different numbers of fingers
pointing upwards for sharps and down for flats, with a
clenched fist for C major. So, for example, three fingers
downwards would signify E♭, three upwards for A, and so
on. You have to be a bit careful with D major, but apart
from that it's fine. I've never found having a maximum of
four fingers to be a great disadvantage with any of the
musicians I've ever worked with, and if you go for the
Vineyard model two will be plenty. So learn your hand
signals, teach them to your non-musical leaders, and
practise them until you can do a 'once-through-the-chorus-
then-up-into-G#-for-a-slow-voice-over-with-some-
singing-in-tongues' with one hand tied behind your back.
You can have great fun in rehearsals trying to catch one
another out, but when you come into the Lord's presence

for real in a service, you'll have such a trust and empathy that nothing you do will interrupt worship for God's people.

To whom do you signal? I'm not sure it's possible to 'conduct' the group as a whole. Even with a smallish group that in itself would be a full-time job, leaving little attention for the congregation or the Spirit. It's probably best, therefore, to be in touch with the player of the most dominant instrument – usually either the keyboard player or a strong guitarist. Designate someone like that as musical director, and, after you've signalled your intentions, leave them to direct. This does, however, leave a major responsibility with the group. First, the director must actually be looking at you in order to see your signals. Two sorts of keyboard players tend to have trouble with this: the pretty bad and the pretty good. The pretty bad pianist is the one who needs to keep his eyes glued firmly on the music, and can only safely lift them to see your by now frantic 'back to verse five' signal as the last chord of the final chorus fades into silence. The pretty good one is the player who is able to put his fingers instinctively on the right notes and for whom the keyboard becomes an extension of his worshipping being, such that he has his eyes firmly shut, while inwardly seeing a vision of several different angels and receiving a word of knowledge about someone in the congregation with athlete's foot. Your 'a bit slower, please' is clearly on an altogether more mundane plane. So, if they possibly can, musicians should learn to watch carefully, especially towards the end of verses; the dominant one watching you, and the rest ready to follow. As you work together more and more as a team, the whole business of signalling will become easier. It does, of course, take a while to get used to, but in time you'll be able to predict what's likely to happen. And this, again, will set free rather than restrict; you'll be far more comfortable listening to the promptings of God's Spirit if you think you'll be able to obey them. If something more complicated feels right, don't panic; do a voice-over. Once, at the end of a song, someone had a prophecy about how God enjoyed our singing love songs to him, but that he also wanted to sing love songs to us. I felt it would be good to respond to that by affirming God's word to us and articulating the fact of our preciousness to him. Now I haven't actually got in my repertoire a hand signal for that one, but it didn't matter. I signalled 'voice-over', and then said something like 'Let's sing that again, but this time we'll focus less on our love for God and more on his for us. The Lord's just told us how much he delights in us, so let's enter into that truth and simply enjoy his love. Let's listen to the instruments and hear in the spirit his love songs for us.'

On another occasion I was leading worship in a large city-centre church. The emphasis was on prayer and intercession, and at one point we were instructed to turn round and face the back. The large west doors were opened, and we were encouraged to pray out over the city which we could now see. I had to round off a few minutes of exuberant prayer with something which would quieten people down ready for the next part of the service, so we began singing quietly 'Be still for the presence of the Lord'. Suddenly it occurred to me that this song, which is usually used in a mood of quiet adoration, could also be a prophetic statement over the city which we were facing. So I gave the musicians a 'voice-over' signal, and encouraged people, while the music continued quietly, to sing the words prophetically over the city centre, telling it and its inhabitants, as it were, to be still and acknowledge the presence of the Lord who most of the time was ignored or blasphemed, to be still from their money-making, their frantic lifestyles, their seeking after all sorts of false gods, their crime, violence, drug-taking and prostitution. The words 'Come bow before him now with reverence and fear' took on new meaning as they became a proclamation to the world rather than an encouragement to the faithful, and the musicians, catching the mood immediately, put a completely different feel into the accompaniment. The prayer was rounded off with a triumphant declaration, and it all happened because we had a hand signal which allowed us to pause and rethink the emphasis and style of the song.

Hand signals only work, of course, if the group has some basic ground rules, and they are not a substitute for lots of hard work on learning how to play songs. We can signal 'repeat the chorus' with the utmost clarity, but unless the musicians know how to do so, it won't work. How many beats, or bars, are there before it starts? These turnarounds will need to be worked out for each song.

So learning a song isn't just about learning it straight through from the book; you then need to go on and learn how to get smoothly back into an extra chorus, a repeat of a verse, or whatever. There aren't really any hard and fast rules about this, but most musicians (and many non-musicians) can 'feel' what's right and what's awkward. Similarly key changes need to be done smoothly, whether you're modulating up a key in the middle of a song to give it a bit of an extra lift, or changing keys between two songs. Extras like these need to be worked on and practised until you can be sure that all the musicians, on seeing a hand signal, will think, 'Oh, that's what he wants us to do,' rather than, 'Help, how on earth do we do that?'[2]

In the planning stage you'll need to have worked out which songs you think will flow uninterrupted together, and at which points you may want to insert some verbal material. We use six different terms for the way in which we flow from one song to the next:

Straight in vocally. This is where the next song comes in without an introduction, and without a change in rhythm or tempo. This method requires a strong vocal lead and a very nifty OHP operator who is aware that this is what you intend to do. If you are using songbooks this one is best avoided except when moving to very well-known songs. Obviously there is little time to shout out the number between the two songs, but you can do so safely once the second one has started. If a key change is involved, it needs to be done swiftly by using the dominant (or fifth) chord of the key you are moving into. This isn't as complicated as it sounds; you should be able to feel whether it is working or not, even if you are not very musical.

Straight in with intro. Here the rhythmic flow is maintained, but instead of singing the first line, it (or the last line) is played as an introduction, allowing people to come in at the right place. This gives a less hurried feel, but introductions should be clear and not too prolonged if the flow is to be maintained. The same rules about modulation apply.

Voice-over. The musicians move straight into the next song and begin playing it quietly while the leader speaks, either to the people, encouraging them on or bringing something from the Lord to them, or to the Lord in prayer, wrapping up and articulating what the people might want to say in response to what they've just sung. Generally speaking, the deeper into adoration you get, the less you'll address the congregation and the more you'll address God. Voice-overs require something of the skill of the disc-jockey in getting the timing right so that the congregation are brought in at a convenient point. It's worth playing through a song beforehand and noting convenient 'access points' where you could stop talking and let the congregation in, and places where you must keep going at all cost. Again, all this sounds very difficult and contrived, but you'll know when it works. (The congregation will know when it doesn't work, because they'll be left hanging in the air wondering when to begin singing. If it flows properly it will have the naturalness and unobtrusiveness which doesn't betray the fact that you spent two hours with the band practising it.)

Reverse voice-over. No, this doesn't mean that you are talking out of the back of your neck. It is exactly the same as a voice-over except that the musicians play through the last song instead of the next one. When you are ready to move on, they will pass smoothly to the introduction to the next song (and to the new key if necessary). A variation of this is to play the old song in the new key. This is slightly more difficult to achieve than the straight voice-over, but it is worth trying occasionally.

Tiny pause. Tiny because you want to break the flow and keep silence, perhaps for a change in mood, but you don't want people to be left wondering if you've fallen asleep or been struck with amnesia. If you want a more prolonged time of silence, that's fine, but you need to let people know that's what you're doing. The tiny pause is different; it's simply a way of getting from one song to the next without complete flow. It is best used sparingly if you want to avoid the stop-start feel of badly led worship, but it can be effective now and then. It can also be a last resort if you simply can't work out the key change involved between two songs.

The planned spontaneous happening. As we've already discussed, this needs to be led in the sense that people need to know what's happening, and that they are expected, rather than just allowed, to contribute. I often come in with a short prayer after a song has ended, and then say something like 'Let's all take some time to thank the Lord as we speak out our praises to him.'

In putting together a list, therefore, the leader will need not just to put down the songs, but also the links. Just as we've developed our hand signals, we've also standardised a set of hieroglyphics which we put on the list to show what we think might happen. Added to this we put down the key or keys we're going to sing each one in, and some instruction about how many times through, and any creative repeating we might attempt! It's important for you to develop terminology and notation which is understood by all those involved with you, and to use it as a basis for your playing together. As with the planning process you can modify or even abandon it when you get really good, but to use it as a kind of apprenticeship is a good discipline, which will give you solid foundations on which to build into the future. It is worth saying that we didn't all sit down one night at a rehearsal and work out how to write lists; our system has evolved over a period of time, and is no doubt still evolving.

Another important point needs to be made here too. It concerns the discovery I made some years ago of the need for 'air-holes'. Because I put a high value on smooth flow in a worship slot, and because I'm always very nervous leading worship, I'd found great security and comfort in planning slick changes from song to song, like all those mentioned above. But I realised to my horror that people were feeling rushed along, almost without breathing space, and that they were finding it difficult to meet God between the songs, and therefore in them. Around this time I went to a meeting where some of the real experts were in action, and I was struck by how much space they left, and how a very powerful worship time could be achieved with half the number of songs I'd have used. I'm not, of course, advocating a return to the 'spontaneous' worship model with its embarrassed silences, but with skilful musicians improvising between songs there can still be a sense of stillness and space – air-holes for people to breathe in God's Spirit. I hope I'm getting better about this. Beware lest your nerves tend to make you rush panting through a list.

Finally, a word on 'prophetic worship'. This is now well-established in the worship scene, although it often feels as if it is beyond the reach of all but the most top-grade bands. Basically it is the ability to sing and play directly from the heart of the Lord, using words and music given by him. Just as in prophecy the person concerned will receive in his mind words from the Lord which he then speaks out, in prophetic worship the words will be put by the 'prophet' to an improvised tune so that the prophecy can be sung, and accompanied by the other musicians. The first time I heard of this concept I just couldn't believe it, and couldn't see at all how it could happen. But having now experienced it many times, I've seen how incredibly powerful it is. A singer and a group of musicians really can improvise spontaneously at the same time and communicate powerfully together what is on the Lord's heart. You just have to know how to get into it.

It is usually based around a fairly simple chord progression which the musicians can lead into when they know that someone feels a prophecy coming on, so that the melody can be improvised over the top. Alternatively the musicians may continue after a song has ended with a simple sequence, perhaps based on the harmonies of the song, providing the opportunity for a singer to launch off, or a singer can begin, with the other musicians drifting in when they have got hold of the key and structure of the tune. It needn't only be a singer, of course. Instrumental prophecy can be very powerful indeed, and can communicate God's heart as effectively as words can.

Before a group can begin to work on this type of worship, individuals within it need to start on their own to build up confidence, through what has been called 'creative worship'. The essence of this is simply to make up songs or tunes, without bothering too much whether it's God or just you. One of the simplest ways is to lock yourself in somewhere soundproof with your guitar or keyboard and a Bible, and simply turn to a psalm at random and sing it. It doesn't matter what it sounds like, and whether the tune is well-structured or whether it takes off and never comes in to land. It doesn't matter whether the Lord is giving you the song or you're making it up: just do it, and keep doing it until you realise that it isn't as impossible as you thought. You may feel that it is appropriate if your randomly chosen psalm is one of those which begins 'Make a joyful noise...'. The first time I tried it I got a really miserable one, with the waters about to engulf me, enemies all around me and my feet in miry clay and sinking fast. I started off feeling fine, but after a few verses of that I virtually needed to go for counselling. Nevertheless, this is a good way to become confident with your own voice, and particularly with improvising with it. Only when some of the group members feel comfortable with this can the group as a whole move into practising corporate improvisation.

If all this sounds a bit unspiritual, think of spoken prophecy; unless a person can actually talk, and can do so out loud without dying of embarrassment, the Lord can try as hard as he likes but will never get a prophecy communicated to his people through that person. In the same way our practising the skills of improvisation can be seen as preparing ourselves in case God ever wants to use us. And, of course, as soon as we are able to be used in that way, we'll find that God does want to use us – frequently.

There is more to prophetic worship, though, than just 'singing a song the Lord's given me' (sometimes when you hear them you can see why the Lord gave them: he desperately wanted to get rid of them); it can be anything which reflects the heart of the Lord during a worship time. Some of the most effective things I've heard have been 'accompanied pictures'; in other words the sharing by someone of a picture or vision they've received while the musicians paint the picture in sound with their instruments, adding to the overall effect considerably. Sometimes the direction of the words can be from us to God rather than vice versa, as our prayers take on a prophetic feel, 'breathing back the breathings of God', as John Wimber has put it. Sometimes the leader can encourage the congregation in this by setting up an 'echo', where he sings a line which is then repeated by the people. No doubt much of the liturgy in the Old Testament began in this way. And sometimes there are no words at all, simply playing which communicates non-verbally and touches people deeply with the touch of God's Spirit. Musicians should learn to play 'creatively', improvising together, drifting in and out of the limelight with all the skills of the best traditional jazz bands, bouncing off one another and above all knowing when to stop. At times the Lord will anoint your creative worship and enable you to play 'prophetically', reflecting his heart and communicating deeply to his people.

Musicians can work on this kind of extempore playing by increasing their musical vocabulary. We all know that minor chords sound sad and solemn, major chords sound happy, and diminished chords sound scary. But a good musician has much more awareness than this basic level of what moods different harmonies and styles can evoke and describe, so that a sound-picture can be painted behind the words which complements and reinforces them very powerfully. The larger your vocabulary, the more things you are able to say, and therefore the more available to the Lord's promptings you will be.

The best thing I've seen written on prophetic worship is the section in Jo King's *Leading Worship*.[3] As well as looking at the spiritual qualities needed in the 'prophet', he gives some very practical musical ideas. The book ends with a series of exercises which can be used by the worship group to help them grow in different aspects of the prophetic and musical ministry. If you feel that you might be ready to begin exploring this area, his book is a must.

Finally, a lesson on how not to encourage people into prophetic worship. At a conference, at about 9.30 in the morning, we began a worship time, and after one song the enthusiastic leader, who must have had a real gifting from the Lord to be that enthusiastic that early in the morning, told us that the Lord wanted us to get into groups of three, face each other, and sing prophetic songs to one another in the groups. Whatever the Lord was giving us for one another, or whatever was on our hearts, we were to sing it out. Imagine the scene! All around the room people fainted, suddenly needed to go to the loo, became instantly paralysed, and so on. Then, loud and clear above the chaos a song rang out from one of our party, beautifully sung with a brilliantly improvised tune and the deeply touching words 'O Lord, let the ground open up and consume me'. If you think that sounds embarrassing, you should have been there when we went back to the church and tried it at the next PCC meeting.

Having worked out your list, all you have to do is lead people in worship using it. Use hand signals either to confirm what you've already decided or to change it; listen to the Spirit; don't talk too much; don't be afraid to leave those air-holes in the context of your smooth flow; be ready for the prophetic; and worship the Lord yourself. Expect God to come and minister to his people, give him space to do so, and you can't go far wrong.

Notes

1 See my chapter in John Gunstone (ed.) *Meeting John Wimber* (Crowborough: Monarch, 1996) pp 151–161.
2 For a lot more detail about these kinds of skills, see Jo King, *Teach Yourself Praise Guitar* (Eastbourne: Kingsway, 1983); *Leading Worship* (Eastbourne: Kingsway, 1988); Stuart Townend, *Playing the Keyboard in Worship* (Eastbourne: Kingsway, 1993) and my own *Hymns and Spiritual Songs* (Cambridge: Grove, 1995).
3 Jo King, *Leading Worship* (Eastbourne: Kingsway, 1988).

10

Handling the Congregation

I've called this chapter 'Handling the Congregation' but I don't want to give the impression for one moment that what we are trying to do is in any way manipulative. Apart from the Lord himself, the congregation are the most important people involved in worship, and we need as leaders to know how to honour and respect them, and to show that we do by the way we lead them. I want to consider first their needs, and secondly what they might do during a worship time, both helpfully and unhelpfully, which might need, in the best sense of the word, 'handling'.

Before I discuss those things, though, we do need to remind ourselves of what it is that the Lord wants to do with his people in worship. First and foremost, I believe, he wants to draw them into his presence and do the sort of things he loves doing and which will make them as individuals and as a congregation more like Jesus, in their ministry and their character – healing, renewing, equipping, and so on. And secondly, he simply wants to enjoy their worship. He wants to accept the gifts they are offering to him gladly and joyfully, as they delight his heart, and he wants to enjoy watching them at worship and their enjoyment of it.

Those of us who are parents will understand a bit about

this dual enjoyment. I can remember well the time when my eldest son (now a teenager) was at the stage of learning to write, and of wanting to send me little cards and pictures for my study notice-board. I received all sorts of little offerings, but my favourite is from his slightly earlier and more 'impressionist' period; it depicts a totally undifferentiated mess of green scribble, and bears at the bottom, in the hand of a helpful adult, the explanatory title 'God help Joseph'. If he looks anything like his picture, he certainly needs all the help he can get. But I got the same twofold enjoyment from Steve's artwork that I believe God gets from our worship; I enjoyed the gift, and the love and relationship which it represented, but I also enjoyed watching him drawing and writing, because I could see from his face the fun he was having doing it, and the sense of pride and achievement when it was finished. My wife had an important role in this process too; she was the one who cleared the table, got the paints or pens out, and restrained Steve's little brother in his attempts to help. She helped with spelling, and finally she cleared up the mess afterwards.

The worship leader's role in all this is, I reckon, pretty similar to that of my wife in the art studio. Someone has to be there to resource the congregation, to make sure there is space for them to worship, to help communication by sometimes having a slightly greater understanding than the average of the congregation, and then, with the ministry team, to clear up any mess created in the process. Leaders are simply the 'service department', keeping things running smoothly and effectively. Everything I say in this chapter should be understood in the light of this attempt, not to manipulate or dominate, but simply to serve the worshipping people of God.

So what is it that they need? One thing, I believe, above all else, and I've mentioned it in a previous chapter – security. I suppose I'd define security in this context as the certainty that everything is going to be OK. Whatever I do, whatever anyone else does, whatever God himself does, it'll be OK. Even if I do something wrong, it'll be OK. God is good, the leader knows what he's doing, everyone here loves me, so it's OK to be a part of it. It may even be OK to do something if I feel right about it; pray out loud, or jump up and down a bit, or something like that. What we're actually after as leaders is seeing everyone in the congregation involved and participating as individuals, and yet creating a corporate dimension which is much more than just the sum of its parts. Without security we won't be able to draw individuals in, and without individuals there'll be no corporate dimension either, and the whole thing will feel like yesterday's Yorkshire pudding.

So security is vital, and we've talked a bit already about how we can help provide it. But along with it come three other ingredients – commitment, expectation and involvement – which are also pretty essential if our worship is regularly going to rise above the mediocre. The three are so closely tied in together that it is difficult to know where to start, but I think they involve respectively a decision of the will to be a worshipper, even if I have to do it in spite of the worship leader and everyone else, a belief that it will be worthwhile, since God will actually meet me and do something, and a decision to contribute something to the corporate nature of the worship experience rather than to keep it all nice and private between the Lord and me. In a previous parish, the staff of our church met from time to time with a group of other church leaders from the area, including several New Church elders. When we began to pray together it was easy to tell who was who; they began instantly with muttering, semi-audible tongues, shouts of 'Hallelujah!' and all the rest of it (one person said it reminded him of the old hymn 'Hoover around us while we pray'), while we Anglicans composed ourselves silently for the time ahead and wondered if when we began to say something we'd be interrupting a real prayer or only an interlude. I remember remarking to a fellow Anglican the first time I heard this carry-on, 'They're so emotional, aren't they?' 'No,' he replied, 'we're emotional; they're committed.' I realised he was right. We were sitting there wondering how we felt, and deciding whether it was going to be a sufficiently good prayer time for us to get into it and get excited about things, while they were just getting on and making it a good prayer time, totally unconcerned about how they may have been feeling. I think that attitude to worship is what I mean by commitment, and the obvious expectancy revealed in their prayers and their desire to be involved publicly with others are traits within the Pentecostal and Restorationist traditions which other churches could do well to learn from, even if they did it a bit more quietly. It certainly is a joy occasionally to lead worship when there is a large New Church contingent present; they're always raring to go right from the very first chord, and it makes the leader's job considerably easier when you have a congregation that committed. It's very different from the usual, when the first few songs can be spent attempting to bump-start the people in a way which feels rather like trying to stir cold tarmac.

Expectancy is something we bring to worship with us, whether we're conscious of it or not. The problem is that it may be either positive or negative. If we arrive to find out that it's *him* on duty to lead worship tonight, our expectancy level may soar into the positive or plummet into the negative depending on our past experience of him. Since all expectancy tends to fulfil itself, the view of him which we have will be reinforced even further. Our moods, as well as the personnel, can affect the way a worship time goes, as can many other factors. Obviously a good dose of commitment will help in the expectancy department, but the fundamental way of raising the level is to concentrate first and foremost on the Lord, and not on ourselves or anyone else around. The more we expect him to do, the more he actually will do; the more he did last time, the more we'll expect him to do this time, and so it goes on. This is honestly not an attempt to psych ourselves up or to kid ourselves with some kind of 'double-think'; it genuinely does work like that. In the past one of my major responsibilities was to lead teams which went out to other parishes to run evenings or weekends for them. I would always tell the clergy at churches which I was about to visit that the single best thing they could do in the run-up to the weekend to prepare people was to work on their expectancy. The whole thing is a bit of a vicious circle, so it's better to have a positive vicious circle (if you can have such a thing) which spirals upwards than a negative one which goes the other way.

Involvement, thirdly, is important if the worship is to be more than a performance by the person at the front. It is a conscious decision to be a part of what is going on, to look a part of what is going on, and even at times to do something which may affect what is going on. Whether it means contributing a prayer, a prophetic word, a picture, or whatever, or just joining in fully in the worship of the whole congregation, it is essential to the flow of good worship. Depending on the size of the gathering in question, it may be more or less easy for someone to contribute in some kind of a publicly vocal way, and a church should, of course, have some form of small groups where people can learn gradually to contribute out loud in a less threatening atmosphere, but it is still necessary for the worship leader to get some kind of a sense of the people's willingness to be involved in the activity in question. It can make all the difference if your congregation is good at this, and one way to tell how good they are is to watch what happens between songs rather than during. If people switch out of 'worship' mode and into 'looking around to see what's going to happen next' mode, the chances are they're not very good in the involvement stakes. But if they remain engaged with the Lord and are very obviously still worshipping even when the music stops, they're the sort of worshippers it'll be a joy to lead. This is once again where the New Church style of worship comes into its own, where every spare moment is filled with praise, uttered enthusiastically and semi-audibly. It really does help the leader to feel that it is not, after all, up to him alone.

What makes the difference? Essentially it has to do with whether or not people are used to being worshippers on their own. Those who regularly come before the Lord in praise and adoration in their own devotional times will feel happy with doing so publicly, and won't mind too much whether or not there happens to be a song going on at the time. But the insecure people, who feel a bit lost when things aren't happening up front, can often be those who find solo worship difficult. Leading worship in a large gathering with a high proportion of such people is very hard work; trying to do it in a small home group is disastrous. Above all, leaders need to work on equipping people for their own individual worship. Strong, committed, expectant, involved worshippers, when put together in a crowd, will make for exciting and moving worship.

What sort of things, then, might people from the congregation do during a time of worship? It is worth saying right from the start that a worship leader is dealing with a very varied collection of people in any congregation, and their contributions will vary considerably too. They will range from the stunningly powerful prophecy which stops the whole event in its tracks, right through to the disastrously inappropriate outburst of demon-inspired screaming and blasphemous obscenities. Both extremes and everything in between need careful handling if the best is to be made of them, and it is a very skilled job indeed to be able to do this well. So let's look at some possibilities. This is, of course, not an exhaustive list. Human beings are much more creative than that!

1. Sentences of praise

It's helpful sometimes to give people the space to respond in a personal but public way to what's going on musically or liturgically. So, for example, after singing a song focusing on God's goodness, it might be good for you to encourage people to speak out particular aspects of God's goodness which have struck them especially over the last week. People might respond with one-sentence prayers like 'Thank you, Lord, for your provision for our needs', 'Thank you, Father, for your healing power' and so on. Not only is this good because it is a way of encouraging one another, but also because it gives people the chance to express personal thanksgiving in the context of the whole congregation in a way which is honouring to God. And also, if we're honest, it probably encourages some people actually to give thanks to God. They may well have taken things for granted, but have now had a prod and an opportunity to 'count their blessings'. The same principle can be effective further on in worship, when in the middle of a phase of intimate adoration people can be encouraged to speak out their words of love and devotion to the Lord. It can be an awesome experience to share with one another that deeply.

Training a congregation into sentences of praise may take a bit of time, since it may be a new way of praying which requires one of two equal and opposite new skills. The first is simply to be able to pray out loud in that way, and this will be difficult in churches where everything has been led very much from the front before now. Again small groups could be very helpful here, as could a bit of modelling from you and one or two 'plants' in the congregation whom you have previously warned. The shorter the prayer, the easier it should be, and to encourage people to 'break the sound barrier' and do it for the first time can be a very helpful thing for them which will be important in lots of different areas of their Christian experience. My wife and I have written elsewhere about how to get young children praying out loud, and people have told us that the guidelines suggested work exceptionally well with adults too.[1]

Some people, though, will have the opposite problem, and will not need asking twice to get going with their long, theologically exact prayers, which cover everything from the needs of their Auntie Gladys and her varicose veins to the plight of the church in Papua New Guinea and back again. Not only does this distract from the real task in hand, which is to give praise to the Lord, but it also alienates other people and makes it impossible to draw the less confident into praying, since they may well feel that they need at least to match the verbosity of the previous prayer, and that the 'Thank you, Lord, for your love to me' which they had up their sleeve is nowhere near stunning enough. I'm not implying at all that the more prolix prayers are in any way insincere, just a bit unhelpful in this context. The leader of worship may need to do something to restrain people, first of all, as we've said, by modelling brief prayers, and then, if necessary, by gently insisting on 'one sentence' prayers. He needs to be able to give clear instructions as to what he is inviting the congregation to do, without intruding on the sense of worship which has been reached. In extreme cases someone in authority may even need to have a quiet word afterwards with the offending party to explain that their contributions, although ideal in another setting, may not have been the most helpful thing for that particular time. So, although there are dangers here, used properly such verbal interjections can have a boosting effect on the worship.

2. Spiritual gifts

One of the more positive aspects of renewal is the rediscovery of the priesthood of all believers. The Reformers fought so hard for this, and yet were unable to bring it about functionally. Now we are used to the Lord speaking through anyone in the congregation by means of prophecy, tongues and interpretation, pictures, and so on. There is no doubt that this is generally a positive step forward, but it is not without its dangers. It seems to me that we can often fall down in one of two ways, and great skill is needed in testing and in responding. Let's have a look at each of these.

The Bible is very clear that any so-called manifestation of the Spirit should be weighed up in order that the congregation is not led astray by something which appears to be from the Spirit but actually is not. There are enough accounts of false prophecy in the Bible to make us all aware of the dangers inherent if it is not checked out properly. I find it helpful to think of the testing process as having two main stages. First of all, the person who thinks he is 'getting' something should test it out himself. Commonly what happens is that he will begin to feel physical sensations in his body (heat, thumping heart, hair on end, etc.) followed by the impression of a few words on his mind, which, if spoken out, will be replaced by a flow of words given a bit at a time. His first task, therefore, if he thinks that what he is experiencing is the Lord and not just the Gorgonzola he had for lunch, is to pray silently something like, 'Lord, if this is not from you, please take it away.' Sometimes exactly that will happen, and his mind will go blank, leaving not even the memory of what it was he was going to say. But more commonly the words will return with even more force. The more timorous charismatic may like to repeat the process to be absolutely sure: 'Lord, really, I mean it... please take this away if it's not right for me to say it!' Doing this much more than twice will usually be counterproductive, so after that it's best to go for it anyway. There is still the second part of the testing process, which involves the church, meaning, in practice, the worship leader.

The leader, having heard the 'prophecy' or whatever, needs to ask five questions:

(i) Who is the prophet?

While wanting to be as positive as we can, giving everyone the benefit of the doubt, there are some people who we know have a particular agenda which they lose no opportunity of broadcasting. Others may simply be unknown to us – perhaps visitors who are hearing God correctly and have a message for us, but alternatively they could be weirdos who have wandered in off the street. Particularly if the 'word' is negative or critical, it will be much more believable as genuine if the person bringing it is known to us as someone of great insight or discernment. Common courtesy demands that visitors do not speak prophetically to a congregation they are not a part of without very good reason and careful testing along other lines.

(ii) Is it scriptural?

Does it tie in with what the Bible reveals of the character of God and his dealings with us? Is it the sort of thing which God would say? If not, it must be suspected of being wrong. Some of you may have been at the famous Fountain Trust meeting many years ago when someone said, as from the Lord, that Roman Catholics and women who wore trousers were an abomination to him. Not only was this suspect because neither trousers nor Roman Catholics get a significant mention in the Bible, but more importantly because our God just wouldn't say things like that. At least, that's what the leadership at the time thought. I'm inclined to agree with them.

(iii) Is it positive?

It seems to be a characteristic of biblical prophecy that it always leaves what has been called 'a door of hope'. It is Satan's way of working to back us into a corner from which there is no escape, while God, on the other hand, wants to lead us out into freedom. Therefore a 'prophecy' which is all about our sin, wickedness and degradation is to be suspected if it doesn't go on to say something like '…therefore repent and turn back to me, and I will wash you clean from your sin…' at the end. A totally negative word is not from the Lord. God may indeed have to say hard things to his church at times; that of itself does not make it false, but if it simply leaves people feeling guilty and battered, it is definitely out of order.

(iv) Is it right?

Does it fit in with the context of what God seems to be doing at the time? If not, it's probably right to forget it. I was leading a worship workshop once, and during an open praise session between two songs someone piped up about how we should not be singing praise just in church, but should be doing it outside in the streets as a witness to the unsaved. While this was no doubt true, I didn't feel too good about it, but left it without saying anything. But when the same person spoke out again later, along similar lines but much more vehemently, about what was the good of this noise if only the saved could hear it, I felt it right to step in and stop him, on the grounds that God was not challenging us to evangelism right now, but was teaching us to worship. What God was leading us into was not 'noise', but praise which he really valued from his children. My point is that in another context that word may have been exactly right, but just not then.

(v) Is it anointed?

Sometimes you can just tell after a word has been given that there was real power in it. You can see from the faces of people in the congregation that it has 'cut them to the heart', and the almost stunned silence which follows speaks clearly of the effect which the Spirit is having on the lives of those who heard. But at other times a word can be very scriptural, positive and contextually correct, but still give you the impression of having left the person's mouth and trickled down their chin and into their top pocket. Somehow the right words just seem to lack any power behind them. This is not a function of how vehemently they were spoken, but much more of the lack of the Spirit's authority behind them.

What do you do, then, if a 'prophecy' fails one or more of these tests? I think you have to ask where the word did come from, if not from God. In most cases it will have come from misguided human enthusiasm, linked sometimes with a slightly unstable personality. An article in *Theological Renewal* some years ago identified three types of 'false prophet': the 'Demagogue', who is obsessed by power and considers himself untouchable and beyond any testing; the 'Railer', who works very much from his own emotional agendas; and the 'Deceiver', who attempts to spread wrong doctrine and confusion. Tom Smail added to these three a fourth category, the '"Prattler of Pious Platitudes", in whose hands the two-edged sword of the word is blunted and turned into a butter knife or a jam-spreader'.

When, in one of our services, someone told us that the Lord said we were a load of hypocrites, we were able to discern very quickly that it was purely the girl in question reflecting her opinion of the church – an opinion which was no secret to anyone. She was acting as a 'Railer'; the other categories are similarly easy to spot. Unless the person is being a nuisance or articulating wrong doctrine which needs to be corrected, these types of words are best left uncommented upon, perhaps with a private chat afterwards if they do it repeatedly. Most often the congregation themselves will be the best judge of such words, since they will have forgotten them within about three minutes.

The same applies to what I can only refer to as 'low-grade' words, the kind of thing which is very nice but has little effect. 'My children, I love you' may be just what the congregation needs to hear at that time, but often will simply leave people feeling 'Yes... that's nice....' If you do need to say anything negative about a word, remember that the idea is to shut the person up and to protect the congregation from possible error, but to do so in a way which is loving to the person and which does not freeze any other potential prophets with terror in case they blow it too. Such phrases as 'I'm sure that's right, but I'm not so sure that's what the Lord is doing at the moment...' or 'I think the Lord would want to be a bit more positive than that towards us...' are probably more effective than outright confrontation, and can leave the person feeling 'Good try, nearly got it right,' instead of 'Oh no! I'm a false prophet possessed by an unclean spirit!'

At times you may run into what you consider to be a deliberate satanic counterfeit of prophecy, and this will need praying against specifically and the person will need rebuking more strongly (and not uncommonly ministry for deliverance) but this is pretty rare. Most times it is simply human nature, not the Enemy. The gift of discernment is obviously vital here, and as you get more experienced you will rely less on these five questions (although they still form a useful framework) and much more on how you *feel* about the word, and about the 'prophet'.

If, however, as is far more likely, the word does feel OK, you then have another problem – what do you do with it? The area of responding to the word requires a similar amount of skill on the part of the leader. We have all experienced times when a word has really got to us, but we are then rushed into the next song with no chance to take it on board. Often what is needed is simply some space to respond personally, so an invitation to keep silent for a few minutes and allow time for the Lord to apply the word to our hearts is appropriate. At other times we may need to act in response to what the Lord has said, and our worship may need to change dramatically and go off in a new direction, for example penitence. This is where the skilful worship group comes into its own, as musicians are able at a moment's notice to begin a song which is not on the list but which leads people in the direction which is appropriate. By the time the leader has said, 'Let's respond to the Lord's call to humble ourselves before him,' the musicians (who have carefully rehearsed their default mode) will already be playing the introduction to a suitable song. Thus the flow is not broken, even though the direction may have suddenly changed. Or perhaps the word will have spoken to individuals rather than to the congregation as a whole, and there may be the need to invite people to receive ministry, either then or at the end of the service. There may be several options, but the leader will have to ensure that some response is made, otherwise the effect of the word will be lost. When the Lord really speaks, it's not an option to press on regardless. Much of what I have said in my book *Responding to Preaching* has application in this area also.[2]

3. Spontaneous songs

Sometimes, even in the most well-planned worship time, the congregation, or rather someone from it, will want to take over, and may suggest, or even start up, a song. How do you handle that? It is worth remembering that this is basically a good thing, even though it may cause you inconvenience at times. You are there, after all, to facilitate the worship of the people, so if they do actually start worshipping in this way, it is to be welcomed, since it shows that you are doing your job properly. However, you do need a bit of discernment here. Does the song fit with the flow of where you are going? If it does, fine – go for it.

There is one law here which I have found to be almost universally true; I am even tempted to call it 'Leach's Law'. It states that a worship song started from the congregation will always be started in a key with the highest possible number of sharps or flats. Really skilful people can even at times excel themselves and go for quarter-tones. I remember our pianist once shrugging her shoulders and pointing despairingly at the little crack on the keyboard between the B and the B♭ while the congregation were lustily but unaccompaniedly singing 'I love you Lord'. Even with a tuneable synthesiser it's next to impossible to help them out in a situation like that! So what can you do? You need brilliant timing to be able to wait until the gap between the first and the second time through, and then to thump out the dominant chord of the key you should be in to lead them to the right place for the repeat of the song. If you can play in A# minor, fine, but if you do need to modulate, that's a helpful way to do it without breaking the flow.

But what if the song is totally inappropriate? If someone shouts out during the gap between 'Lord you are so precious to me' and 'I just want to praise you', 'Can we sing "The Happy Song"?' a good stock answer is 'Yes, but not now!' (If you can actually remember to fit it in later on that's good, but don't feel you have to.) But if they are even braver and just start singing it, there's not a lot you can do, except make no attempt to accompany them and let it die after the first verse. Then you can get back to what you were doing before you were interrupted. The chances are that everyone else in the congregation will feel the inappropriateness of it as much as you do, and will very quickly settle back into the direction they were going in before. Let me emphasise again that basically participation is a positive thing, but it does have to be handled properly if it is to be as effective as possible.

4. Clapping

And why not? If the song demands it, people may begin to clap along in time. You just need to watch the dramatic tempo changes you rehearsed so carefully. Unless you give a clear indication of what you're going to do, you may have a burst of what sounds like machine-gun fire from the congregation. And a song which gradually speeds up is liable to go completely over the top if the congregation gets too free a hand (or should I say, pair of hands?). The musicians, and not the congregation, need to be in control of the tempo. But apart from those obvious difficulties, clapping can be really exhilarating. Also it can be good at the end of a particularly rousing song of celebration when a spontaneous burst of applause breaks out. It's so obviously the Lord who is being clapped that I don't see any danger of removing the spotlight, as it were, from him.

5. Shouts

Graham Kendrick's 'March for Jesus' material has popularised what some churches have been doing for years – shouting in worship. Like clapping, this can be an exhilarating experience, suited particularly to those times when you are concentrating on warfare or proclamation. You just need to make sure that the people know what it is they are supposed to be shouting (usually by getting them to repeat words after you) and that they are given a strong lead from the rest of the worship group which encourages them to bellow out with all their might. There is nothing more uninspiring than a 'festal murmur'.

6. Singing in tongues

Often this will happen almost spontaneously after a song has ended, most commonly a song which is about intimate adoration but has a bit more power to it than some of the quieter ones. There is a strange dynamic about tongues-singing whereby you usually either make it or you don't. There seems to be a sort of threshold sound level above which people cannot hear themselves singing, so that they feel unembarrassed about joining in loudly, which, of course, raises the sound level even more. But if the threshold is never reached, the overall sound is thin and weedy, which in turn makes people sing more quietly lest their contribution actually gets heard. So a good strong lead from the worship group and others who have got over their self-consciousness is important if it is to take off. When it does work, however, there is real power in a time of free praise. I suspect it is a time when people do get healed or touched by the Spirit most commonly, and it is also helpful for those not yet released in tongues, some of whom 'get it' for the first time. It can either be unaccompanied, or the musicians can improvise quietly and sensitively around the tonic chord. Sometimes it can be more structured, as when the leader suggests that people sing their own words for one verse or chorus of a song. You need to make sure that you are not being exclusive to people who don't speak in tongues by saying something like '...in tongues or in English...' when you are giving instructions for free praise.

7. Dance

I have to admit to being somewhat ambivalent here. Many people claim that the charismatic movement has done something important in rediscovering the physical nature of Old Testament worship and reintroducing dance, but I'm never quite sure whether that's true or whether, like the old sacrificial system, dance in worship is something rather messy from the old dispensation from which we've been redeemed now that we live under grace. When done well, liturgical dance can be profoundly moving and can say things which mere words can only hint at. But quite honestly the sight of 400 people jumping up and down on the spot does nothing for me at all. I suppose I find it most effective when choreographed to fit a particular piece of music (I remember particularly a dance my wife produced one Easter to taped music of Elton John's 'Funeral for a Friend', which had me in tears), but much less helpful in the context of what this book would call 'worship'. It can look very clichéd (I love the description of liturgical dance as 'synthetic ecstasy dressed by Laura Ashley'), and like all art forms, it does require a lot more skill than people think if it is to be effective. Fashions change, and flags, ribbons and sticks come and go, with varying degrees of helpfulness in worship.

Still, if people want to do it they're welcome. I find it a healthy trend that it is increasingly going on at the back rather than at the front of the church, which speaks much more of people's physical offering of praise to the Lord than of exhibitionism. I would certainly want to encourage people to use their bodies much more in their private devotional lives, and it is therefore natural that this should overflow into public praise. As a worship leader you should be prepared for it (I was once nearly put off my stroke on the guitar when a very dapper little man in a smart suit suddenly leapt over three seats and began to stalk and gyrate across the front of the church at high speed like a clockwork toy with an overwound spring), but I can't imagine myself ever wanting to put any pressure on anybody to do it. Maybe I have yet to be 'released' into dance; I don't know, but I'm neither in a hurry for that to happen nor, alternatively, would I want to stop anyone else.

8. The demonic in worship

I put this here, not because I feel it has any connection at all with point No. 7 above, but because it is something which happens in the congregation from time to time and it needs handling by the person up front. We have mentioned already that God ought to meet with us as we worship, and that at times his presence will provoke demonic spirits to manifest themselves. This may happen in various ways, as it did in Jesus' time, with sudden shouting out, perhaps of obscenities, screaming, animal noises, or physical contortions, occasionally of a quite violent nature. The first time this happens it can be quite a shock (especially if it's one of the worship group). As the leader you need to get over the first impression that it's somehow personal. No, it's not your guitar playing that's making them scream; it's the Lord. The great sense of relief which comes over you when you realise that should help you to cope.

One fundamental rule is that the one person who should never get involved in dealing with the demonised person is the one leading worship. Your role is at the front, providing security for the congregation, reassuring them that this is perfectly OK, that you've seen it hundreds of times before, that we can handle it with no problem. Never mind that you're absolutely terrified; just keep smiling and announce the next song. Meanwhile the ministry team will have moved in and moved the person out, to minister to them out the back somewhere. I find it tremendously helpful to remember that when a demon manifests it is good news, not bad, because it can then be dealt with. I'll never forget John Wimber at a conference during a particularly noisy ministry session stalking around the stage beaming and saying 'I love it when demons scream – it's music to my ears!' People were being set free, and that's what mattered. (By the way, don't think that being a worship leader lets you off the hook entirely in the deliverance ministry; you should still know how to handle it, but just not when you're supposed to be at the front.)

I hope this chapter hasn't sounded too negative. The

congregation can be a real nuisance at times in worship, but after all they are the real thing, not us. We're just there to help them, not the other way round. It's another valuable and sadly true insight of John Wimber's that the average pastor basically dislikes and resents his flock, since it gets in the way of what he is trying to do. It would be tragic if worship leaders fell into the same trap. We do well to listen to Paul's advice to his Philippian friends:

> In humility consider others better than yourselves. Each of you should look not only to your own interests, but also to the interests of others (Phil 2:3–4).

We then need to put that into practice in the way we lead them into God's presence in worship.

Notes

1 John and Chris Leach, *And for Your Children* (Crowborough: Monarch, 1994) pp 56ff.
2 John Leach, *Responding to Preaching* (Cambridge: Grove, 1997).

11

Creating Liturgy

We've looked at what liturgy is, why it's important, and how we might use it to the full. I've tried to show that liturgy and renewal need not be enemies, and that rather than restricting our worship it can enable and strengthen it. In my attempts to sell you liturgy I may even have succeeded. You may have become convinced, if you don't already worship through it, that it might just hold the potential for doing you good. And if you are in a liturgical church, you may have picked up some hints about making it even better. But where do we go from here? Does that mean we all have to join the Church of England?

No, it doesn't (although I can highly recommend it!). Whatever your worship style, an awareness of the liturgical can enhance it if you'll let it. So, for all those of you who are definitely not Anglicans, but might just want to become liturgical, I want to end with a chapter on creating your own liturgy.

I have a friend who works for a church newspaper, who sends me, every now and then, various books to review. They vary tremendously in their style, quality and appeal, but there is no doubt which one has been most fun to read and write about. Entitled *Human Rites*, it is simply a collection of liturgical texts for all sorts of life's little experiences.[1]

And they are all here: celebrating a birth; house blessing; blessing a couple (gender unspecified); rituals for abortion; a liturgy for your daughter's first period; a hymn to God our Mother, and my particular favourite, a service for 'coming out of the Baptist ministry in protest at their guidelines on sexuality'. They never put stuff like this in *Patterns for Worship*!

However, in spite of what you may be thinking, the book does actually contain some really excellent liturgy. More important still, though, is the way it encourages us to use liturgy to mark various transition points in life with friends and colleagues around us as we bring to God each part of our journey with him. Anthropologists tell us of the importance of public 'rites of passage', but our culture so often encourages us to take things and hide them away privately inside ourselves. Might this be one contributing factor to the amount of neurosis in our society?

So I want to take you through a process by which you might create and use your own liturgy. At the very least this can be great fun, and it may even help you and your home group, your family or your church to celebrate in ways which will add to the richness of your life together.

1. What's your event?

Liturgies such as those in *Human Rites* are almost always to do with times of change, as are our more familiar rites of passage such as christening,[2] marriage and funerals. There is something about change which lends itself to liturgical celebration: we have already noted how liturgy can communicate the passage of time and gather together past and future into the present. So what important changes are on the horizon for you or those close to you? Probably many. As I write we have a son soon to be confirmed, a friend recently diagnosed as having terminal cancer, a book about to be published and another (this one, in fact) in preparation, a twentieth wedding anniversary approaching, and no doubt many more 'occasions' in the offing. So much of this might helpfully be marked with some kind of ceremony. No doubt there are changes around you too, and you won't need much ingenuity to think of ones which you could work with.

2. What do you want to say?

Remember the infant dedication I described earlier? The problem was that the service seemed to be very unclear about what it was trying to do. So having decided on your event, you need next to think through what exactly it is about that event that you want to say. Let's take a change of job. There are all sorts of possibilities, such as thanksgiving to God for finding you one after years of unemployment; thanksgiving for promotion; sadness because ill health has forced you to step down to a quieter position; apprehension because it is so much more of a challenge; dedication to making a Christian stand right from day one; concern for the family left behind as you spend more time on business trips. There is so much you might want to say. This needs thinking through carefully if your service is not to be ambiguous or vague.

3. What do you want to do?

We have already mentioned the value of ceremonial in worship. Are there liturgical actions which could be a part of your celebration? Life is full of little actions: the ceremonial tearing up of 'L' plates on passing your driving test; the blowing out of candles on a birthday cake; carrying a bride over the threshold of your first home, and many more. What could you do, as well as say, and how could others be involved in the doing of it with you?

4. Does the Bible say it?

A Christian liturgy will no doubt include Bible readings. Where is there a passage on the subject which expresses what it is you want to say? Some occasions will be easier than others to find in Scripture. There are, for example, new babies popping out all over the place, but a liturgy to celebrate the upgrading of your 386 to a Pentium could pose a bit more of a problem. It might provide you with some harmless fun trying, but in my experience it can be a very valuable thing to 'search the Scriptures' in this way to find underlying principles rather than just superficial textual similarities. If the word 'Pentium' doesn't actually appear in the Bible (which, according to my concordance, it doesn't) we have to look more deeply for biblical truths which we might want to apply to this momentous event. This earthing of your service in Scripture will set it firmly within the Christian tradition, and ensure that theological content is added.

As well as specific Bible readings, don't forget that you can use biblical ideas and images in your prayers and praises, as in fact much liturgy and many worship songs do. Don't worry about adapting the text slightly for liturgical use – I recently used a version of Psalm 103 at the start of a service as a responsive dialogue of praise. The psalm moves frequently between second and first person forms ('you' and 'we'), so I altered it so that the service leader's sections were all 'you' and the congregation's 'we', as in this short extract:

> ... who forgives all your sins
> and heals all your diseases,
> who redeems your life from the pit
> and crowns you with love and compassion,
> **who satisfies our desires with good things**
> **so that our youth is renewed like the eagle's.**

This is not a verbatim quotation from the psalm, but in spirit it is identical, and therefore, it seems to me, perfectly acceptable for use, and in fact much more helpful in actual use.

5. Do liturgical texts say it?

While we do want to create our own liturgy, there may be points where a reinventing of the wheel is unnecessary, and where existing material might be appropriate to use. If you're not an Anglican, get to know one. There are a few tame ones around, and if you swallow your pride hard enough they may be good enough to help you in your quest. With so much excellent liturgy being written nowadays, there may well be material you could use, if only you can find a guide to help you explore what is available.

6. Say it!

Time for a first draft of your liturgy. Try putting it together, and as you do so, think back to the section on planning worship. Does it have integrity, direction and flow? Is there a logical and theological movement through the service? Does it say what you want it to say, or is it unclear or confused? One of the most common mistakes of inexperienced preachers is lack of focus: rather than making one clear point from a passage, say Jesus the Good Shepherd, there is the temptation to tell the congregation every single thing I know about John chapter 10, or can glean from all the books I've borrowed. It can be the same with home-grown liturgy. Make one or two points, and make them clearly, rather than pulling together a complete biblical systematic theology of your chosen event.

Think through as well any liturgical actions which may be built in, and their logistics. Does it work smoothly, or are there awkward or jarring parts, or unnecessary fiddling around which could be simplified?

When you've arrived at a text you feel pleased with and which you think will work, you're almost there.

7. Polish it

A liturgy which says what you want it to say and which works liturgically and logistically may seem fine, but it may still be lacking something. Good liturgy has an almost poetic quality about it. Check out what you have written for this elusive quality. Consider the following two lines:

My love is like a red rose.

and

My love is like a red, red rose.

That extra 'red' makes all the difference, doesn't it? What about these two sentences:

Get up, move to the front of the church, stretch out your hands, and I'll give you a little bit of bread and a sip of wine.

and

Draw near with faith: receive the body of our Lord Jesus Christ, which he gave for you, and his blood, which he shed for you.

The first is purely functional; the second is devotional. Go through your text again and look for these qualities. What might you want to change? Liturgists often talk of 'resonance', the ability of simple words to strike chords of memory or meaning which will enrich what you are saying and praying, and to evoke deeper meanings in the users.

Can you alter your language to make it richer and more subtle? This stage is often ignored, but it can make all the difference in creating good liturgy.

8. Do it!

Finally use your service to celebrate the occasion it was designed for. Offer to God your thoughts, feelings, regrets, hopes and prayers. Use it with others, so that together you may come to the living God with thanks, praise, confession, or whatever else is appropriate for the occasion. It'll do you all good, and will provide a memorable milestone in your journey through life.

Notes

1 Hannah Ward and Jennifer Wild, *Human Rites* (London: Mowbray, 1995).
2 I refer of course to the secular ceremony of having your baby 'done' by the vicar, and not to Christian baptism, which can be a very different thing!